P9-BZB-737

CONTENTS

1
Introducing Peru

Ancient Inca cities lost in mist-shrouded valleys, dramatic Andean cordilleras, steamy Amazonian jungles, desert landscapes scribed with relics of a vanished civilization, picturesque colonial towns and Pacific beaches combine to make Peru one of the most exciting destinations in the world. This is a country where relics of an ancient pre-Columbian culture abound, overlaid by the veneer of Spanish colonialism, post-independence immigration, and the volatile revolutionary politics of the 19th and 20th centuries.

For the traveller, Peru offers an embarrassment of riches, and although many visitors see no more than the well-trodden **Inca Trail**, the ruins of **Machu Picchu**, colonial **Cuzco** and **Lima**, the country rewards a longer stay and more in-depth exploration. Mountain trails and seemingly unattainable summits, **Amazon** river journeys, surf-pounded beaches with some of the best waves in the world and cities with a vibrant, uniquely Peruvian blend of cultures are here to be discovered. The human heritage ranges from the enigmatic **Nazca Lines** – thought by some deluded souls to be proof of contact with an extraterrestrial civilization – to the Baroque churches and cathedrals founded by Spanish missionary orders and the Andean fastnesses of the Inca empire, and Peru's breathtakingly rich natural heritage ranges from wasteland where rain never falls to tropical rainforest.

And all this variety is crammed into an accessible package. Peru's most important visitor attractions are within easy reach of the capital, Lima, by air, road and rail.

TOP ATTRACTIONS

*** **Machu Picchu:** the classic lost city in the Andes.
*** **Cuzco and the Inca Trail:** colonial beauty and natural splendour.
*** **Lake Titicaca:** an inland sea and a unique culture.
*** **Iquitos and the Amazon:** into the heart of the jungle.
*** **Arequipa:** World Heritage city.
** **Lord of Sipán:** golden treasures from royal tombs.
** **Chan Chan:** mud-brick metropolis.
** **Kuélap:** cloud forest city.
** **Lima:** a vibrant capital.

Opposite: *An Andean woman with her pet baby alpaca.*

FACT FILE

Area: 1,285,216km²
(496,222 sq miles)
Population: 27 million
Capital: Lima
Second city: Arequipa
Highest mountain:
Huascarán (6768m/22,026ft)
Longest river: Amazon
(6437km/4000 miles)
Official languages: Spanish,
Quechua, Aymara
Main religion: Roman
Catholic Christianity
Currency: Nuevo Sol

Below: *Members of
Peru's indigenous
Amazonian peoples
make up only 11% of the
population, but comprise
more than 40 distinct
tribal groupings.*

A mysterious land, unknown to Europeans until the arrival of the Spanish conquistadors in the 16th century AD, Peru is a blend of **cultures**. Despite the most determined efforts of its fanatically Catholic conquerors to wipe out local cultures, a strong undercurrent of age-old indigenous tradition still flows, often erupting in gloriously colourful, hybrid celebrations that merge Christianity with much older influences.

Peru has much in common with three of its South American neighbours. Like Ecuador, on its northern border, Bolivia to the southwest and Chile to the south, it was part of the **Spanish Empire** from the 16th century until the early 19th century. As a result, its primary language is still Spanish and its population is overwhelmingly Roman Catholic. But there are also significant differences between Peru and its neighbours. Unlike Chile, the majority of its people are of pure **Amerindian** or mixed-race (mestizo) descent. Unlike landlocked Bolivia, its Pacific sea coast opens it to maritime influences. And there are even bigger historic, cultural and linguistic differences between Spanish-speaking Peru and its biggest neighbour, Portuguese-speaking Brazil, from which it is separated by the western watershed of the Andes and with which it shares the hinterland of the Amazonian headwaters. Peru has even less in common with its northwestern neighbour, Colombia. Although they share a border almost 1500km (900 miles) long, the border provinces of both countries comprise vast areas of mountainous tropical forest with few roads or settlements.

For many visitors, Peru's biggest and most obvious attraction is its Inca heritage. **Machu Picchu** – lost for centuries in its high Andean valley and rediscovered only in the 20th century – is a wonder of the world, ranking with Egypt's Pyramids or China's Great Wall for sheer impact. The famed **Inca Trail** has become so popular that the Peruvian authorities are now being forced to place limits on the number of people who may use it each year, and other less well-known Inca heritage sites are being proposed as alternatives for visitors.

But if that Inca heritage is Peru's major selling point, the country is also a very popular destination for active holiday-makers, and offers a wide range of **activities** including some of the world's most challenging mountain climbing, kayaking and river rafting, as well as jungle and mountain trekking.

Perhaps surprisingly for a country with a magnificently long **Pacific coastline**, Peru is less well regarded as a beach destination. In part, this is because much of its coast is rugged and windswept. Because of Peru's unique climate, too, its coast is at its least attractive (and is usually shrouded in chilly sea fog) just when the seasonal climate is most favourable for exploring its Andean heritage sights.

Above: Hiking the Inca Trail is Peru's most popular tourist experience but numbers are limited to protect the environment.

THE LAND

Peru is the third largest country in South America, with a land area of 1,285,216km² (496,093 sq miles), making it larger than France, Spain and Germany combined. The terrain ranges from the western **coastal plain**, the *costa*, through the high and **rugged peaks** of the Andes sierra in central Peru, to the eastern **lowland jungle** or selva of the Amazon Basin.

The country has 2414km (1510 miles) of **Pacific coastline**, stretching from its border with Ecuador in the north (only 3.5 degrees south of the Equator) to the Chilean frontier (18 degrees south of the Equator). The **Andes range**, rising to summits of more than 6000m (20,000ft), forms a geographical boundary between eastern Peru and the **Amazon Basin**, source of the world's second longest river. In the southern reaches of

DURATION OF FLIGHTS
Lima–Arequipa: 85 minutes
Lima–Ayacucho: 35 minutes
Lima–Cajamarca: 60 minutes
Lima–Chachapoyas: 90 minutes
Lima–Chiclayo: 60 minutes
Lima–Cuzco: 55 minutes
Lima–Iquitos: 90 minutes
Lima–Piura: 90 minutes
Lima–Puno: 90 minutes
Lima–Trujillo: 50 minutes
Lima–Tumbes: 90 minutes

Above: *The coca plant is the source of the drug cocaine, creating huge profits for criminal cartels.*

the Peruvian Andes, the 'inland sea' of **Lake Titicaca** – one of the largest bodies of fresh water in the world – forms part of the frontier between Peru and Bolivia.

Between the Andes and the Pacific lie a range of landscapes, influenced by a variety of climates and altitudes and allowing an equally wide variety of **crops** to flourish, including sugar cane, cotton, rice and grapes at lower, warmer altitudes, and maize, potatoes, coca (source of the drug cocaine), coffee, tea, cocoa, and tobacco at higher altitudes. However, less than 3% of Peru's total surface area is arable land, and only 0.4% is under permanent crops.

Environmental issues include deforestation (caused by legal and illegal logging), overgrazing and soil erosion on lowland and highland slopes, desert encroachment in the south, and pollution of rivers and coastal waters by run-off from mineral mining and refining and urban sewage systems.

The Cities

Lima, the capital, is by far Peru's biggest and most cosmopolitan city with a sprawl of suburbs and shanty towns surrounding a core of grandiose Spanish Colonial architecture. Lima proper is home to around 3.5 million people within the official city limits, but the total population of the Lima conurbation is estimated at up to seven million. Many of these are recent emigrants from the Andean highlands, driven to the capital to seek work or to escape the fighting between leftist guerrillas and government forces that made rural life dangerous and difficult during the 1980s and 90s. Around 60,000 people, most of them from the Andes and Amazonia regions, fled their homes between 1980 and 2000. Many migrants from the highland regions now live in shanty towns known as *pueblos jovenes* (young villages) with few services, poor health care and little opportunity for education. Others are proud descendants of early Spanish colonists. Lima is a melting-pot city, and is home to people of European, Asian, Middle Eastern and African descent, as well as the mestizo majority.

Lima's port, **Callao**, was originally considered as a separate community, with Lima proper lying some miles inland from the sea and around 150m (492ft) above sea level. The capital has long since expanded all the way to the coast, and Callao is now part of metropolitan Lima.

Peru has no other very large cities. The country's second city is **Arequipa**, an attractive colonial town of around 350,000 people in the southern foothills, which grew rich from silver mining during the colonial era. North of Lima, on the coast, lie a number of smaller commercial towns – **Chimbote**, **Trujillo** (Peru's third largest city), and **Chiclayo** – which grew up as fishing ports and entrepôts for mineral and agricultural exports from the hinterland. **Iquitos**, capital of Amazonia, is a uniquely isolated riverside city in the depths of the jungle and forms the gateway to Peru's remotest regions. **Cuzco**, high in the Andes, is the gateway to Machu Picchu and the Inca Trail and so has become the tourist capital of Peru, with sophisticated hotels, restaurants, shopping and sightseeing.

EL NIÑO

The aridity of the coast is the product of the cold Humboldt Current, which flows parallel to the coast and prevents warm, moist ocean air from reaching the coast. Rainfall is as low as 100mm (4in) annually and coastal mists known as *garua* blanket coastal regions between June and October. Every four or five years, a warm ocean current known as El Niño (the 'Christ Child', because it usually appears around Christmas time) flows from the north, clashing with the Humboldt and generating heavy rain.

Below: *Cuzco, in the high Andes, is Peru's tourism hot spot and the starting point for exploring the heartland of the Inca.*

BIODIVERSITY

Peru is one of the most biodiverse countries in the world with more butterfly, fish and bird species than any other. It has 462 species of mammal, including 35 species of monkey, one of which, the yellow-tailed woolly monkey, is unique to Peru. There are 379 species of reptile and amphibian, most of them found in Amazonia, including the rare black crocodile. And Peru boasts 25,000 plant species – of which 30% are found nowhere else in the world.

The Coast

Peru's long coastline and its rural hinterland are the most densely populated parts of the country, with small fishing and mineral ports dotted along the coast. Much of the coast is bleak and windswept without being visually spectacular, with barren beaches interspersed with grim rocky headlands. The cold offshore current leads to frequent sea fogs, especially between May and October. From the visitor's point of view, therefore, much of the coast is a disappointment. The **northern coastline**, between Tumbes (close to the Ecuadorean border) and Piura, is more immediately appealing, with sandy beaches that stretch for up to 20km (13 miles), white sand, and a warm tropical climate all year round.

The Mountains

The sierra of the Peruvian Andes soars to its highest point at **Nevado Huascarán**, situated 6768m (21,996ft) above sea level – high enough to be snow-capped even at these near-equatorial latitudes.

Below: *Rising more than 6000m (19,686ft) above sea level, the Andean summits are snow-covered throughout the year.*

The Andean range is divided into a number of minor ranges or **cordilleras**, with (from north to south) the Cordillera Vilcabamba, Cordillera Urubamba, Cordillera Vilcanota, Cordillera Carabaya and Cordillera Apolobamba (between Peru and Bolivia) dominating the southern part of the sierra. The Cordillera Blanca, Cordillera Huayhuash, and Cordillera Raura lie closer to the coast, north of Lima, while the Cordillera Central and the Cordillera Yauyos lie around 100km (64 miles) inland of the capital. Deep river valleys flow westward towards the Pacific from these ranges.

In the Arequipa region of southern Peru, **rivers** have carved valleys more than 3500m (11,600ft) deep into the soft volcanic rock, and vulcanism has also endowed this part of the country with a number of hot mineral springs.

In the north, the Cordillera del Condor forms part of Peru's border with Ecuador, while the Cordillera Azul lies between the Andes and the forests of Amazonia.

Above: *River boats, like this one on the Tambopata River, replace road and rail transport in the vast jungle expanses of the Amazonian region.*

The Jungle

The jungle region of **Amazonia** is the least populated, the least visited and the least developed in Peru, with only a scattering of small settlements along river banks. There are few roads, and the only practical means of transport are air and water, with the Amazon and its tributaries providing a natural system of waterways. Two huge river systems, the **Río Ucayali** and the **Río Marañón**, flow out of the Andes watershed, meeting around 100km (64 miles) west of Iquitos. Roughly 80km (50 miles) east of Iquitos, they are joined by a third tributary, the **Río Napo**, thus forming the **Amazon**, which flows eastward to cross the Brazilian border around 320km (200 miles) east of Iquitos.

Until the advent of air transport in the 1930s, **Iquitos**, capital of Peruvian Amazonia, was much more accessible by river from the Brazilian city of Manaus, far down the Amazon, than from Lima. Logging, mining and agriculture have made inroads into this once pristine jungle region, but the forests of Amazonia still shelter elusive indigenous tribes people and a wide range of unique wildlife.

The Desert

The pocket desert wilderness of **Ica Province** is the result of a unique combination of factors – including

---

GEOGRAPHICAL DIVERSITY

Climatologists say that 28 of the 32 types of climate found on planet Earth can be found within Peru's borders, along with 84 of the planet's 117 life zones. Peru ranks eighth in the world for total forest area, with 13% of the tropical forests of the Amazon region. In the Arequipa region, the Colca and Cotahuasi canyons are the world's deepest. Most of the world's highest navigable lake, Titicaca, is also in Peruvian territory, as is the source of the world's longest river, the Amazon.

Above: *Highways through the Andean cordilleras must traverse high mountain passes*

ALEXANDER VON HUMBOLDT (1769–1859)

The cold ocean current that governs Peru's coastal climate owes its name to the Prussian geographer Alexander von Humboldt, who visited Peru in 1802, travelling more than 1200km (745 miles) in the coastal regions and across the Andes to the Chamaya and Marañón headwaters and making one of the first detailed records of the flora, fauna and geography of Peru in his *Diary of a Journey* and *Pictures of Nature*. Unlike many of his contemporaries, Humboldt was not state-financed, which makes his achievement all the more remarkable.

the presence of cold oceanic currents and the rain-shadow effect of the mountains inland – that unite to deprive this coastal region of any rainfall. The totally arid microclimate has preserved the mysterious **Nazca Lines**, centuries-old relics of a vanished people.

Climate

Peru's climate varies widely according to season, altitude and longitude, from **tropical** in the north and west to **dry desert** in the south and **temperate** to **frigid** in the Andes. **Lima** and the southern and central coast have two clearly defined seasons: summer between October and April, with warm sunshine and no rain, and winter between May and September, with high humidity and drizzling rain. **Cuzco** and the Andes are, unfortunately for the visitor who wants to see all of Peru, the other way around, with a rainy season from December to March and a dry season from May to August, when nights and early mornings are extremely cold. The **Inca Trail** has two seasons: a dry season from April to October and a rainy season, with heavy cloud, from November to March. Average annual temperature at 3000m (9843ft) is around 17°C (63°F) and snow falls at higher altitudes.

Amazonia has a less variable climate, with high heat and humidity, cool nights and torrential downpours at any time of year – and an even wetter rainy season from April to October. Temperatures in the Amazon region average between 25ºC (77ºF) and 30ºC (86ºF) and annual rainfall ranges from 2500mm (98in) to 3500mm (138in).

Trujillo, **Sipán** and the north coast have sun all year round and are hottest from December to March, while the southern desert is hot and dry all year round, with no rain.

Fauna

Peru's diversity of climates and environments provides habitats for an equally rich and diverse array of flora and fauna.

Emblematic of the Andes is the magnificent **Andean condor**, with a wingspan of up to 3m (10ft) enabling it to soar for vast distances. The **llama** – a South American member of the camel family – is at home at higher altitudes, where it lives wild and is also domesticated as a pack animal. The **alpaca**, a relative of the llama, is also domesticated for its extremely fine, warm wool. **Spectacled bears**, **pumas**, and **chinchillas** are also found in upland regions. The **Andean cock-of-the-rocks**, with its vivid orange crest and head, is one of the most colourful bird species of the region.

The **marine ecosystems** of the Peruvian coast are equally biodiverse, and national parks and reserves such as the **Paracas National Reserve**, near the city of Pisco, provide a haven for **flamingos**, **pelicans**, **penguins**, **dolphins**, **sea lions** and many more marine creatures. Further offshore, **sperm whales**, **humpback whales** and **grey whales** also migrate through Peruvian coastal waters.

The rainforest of Amazonia is home to an enormous variety of bird, insect, mammal and reptile species, including

GUANO

The rich, cold waters of the Pacific draw millions of sea birds which roost on a scattering of offshore islands known as the 'guano archipelago' from the Spanish word for bird droppings. Over time, the greatest density of sea birds on the planet deposit tons of nitrate-rich guano on these islands and along the Pacific coast of Peru and Chile. In the 19th century, with nitrates in growing demand for fertilizer and industrial processes, these became a hugely profitable resource – and Chile and Peru even went to war over the nitrate territories.

Below: *The alpaca, a member of the camel family, is kept for its fine wool and tasty meat.*

HARVESTING WATER

Water is precious in Peru's arid coastal regions, and the Inca developed sophisticated methods of harvesting rare rainfalls. With financing from the **Global Environment Facility**, an international agency that helps sustainable development projects in developing countries, fields consisting of raised ridges around 10m (33ft) wide alternating with shallow canals are being reintroduced in the regions where the Inca first used such techniques centuries ago.

the **anaconda**, one of the world's largest snakes and capable of reaching up to 10m (30ft) in length. The Amazon and its tributaries also shelter giant **river otters**, **caimans**, shoals of bloodthirsty **piranha** fish, **giant catfish**, **stingray** and **electric eels**. The **jaguar**, the largest mammal predator in South America, lives in remoter forest areas, which also shelter **sloths**, **tapirs**, and a number of monkeys such as **spider monkeys**, **howler monkeys**, several types of **marmoset**, numerous other mammal species and dazzling bird life such as flocks of **scarlet macaws** and other **parrots**.

Plant Life

Perhaps the most notorious member of Peru's native fauna is the **coca bush**, which flourishes in the cooler slopes of the Andes and has been cultivated here for centuries. Coca leaves, when chewed or brewed into a tea, release alkaloid chemicals that relieve tiredness and alleviate the symptoms of altitude sickness. They

can also be processed to yield the drug cocaine – a much more powerful and addictive stimulant and anaesthetic.

Despite its apparently harsh climate, the Andes range supports a surprising variety of plant species, with lush vegetation and dense **tropical flora** up to 3000m (10,000ft) and more above sea level, especially on the wetter eastern side of the range.

Cloud forest gives way to moorland at around the 4000m (12,000 ft) level.

Cactus, **thorn trees**, and other plants adapted to arid conditions grow in the coastal regions, flowering during the damper season.

Palms and other tropical plants flourish along the Pacific shoreline, with **mangrove swamps** on the tropical northern coast, and in Amazonia **orchids** and **bromeliads** struggle for space beneath giant **baobab** trees, **mahogany** and **cedar**, and **chinchona**, with bark that yields the antimalarial drug quinine.

In a completely different environment, the vast **reed beds** around the shores of Lake Titicaca provide villagers with the raw material for houses and remarkable reed boats (*see* panel, page 99) and floating islands.

Above: *The Amazonian rainforest is home to goblet fungi, denizens of the forest floor.*
Opposite: *Squirrel monkeys are among the most commonly seen primate inhabitants of the rain forest canopy.*

HISTORY IN BRIEF
Earliest Civilizations

The **Inca** civilization was the last – and best known – of more than 10 earlier cultures which flourished in the Andes over a period of some 4000 years before the arrival of the Spanish conquistadors in 1531.

Nineteenth-century archaeologists tended to attribute all the relics of these lost civilizations to the Inca, whose empire in fact lasted only a few hundred years. More recent research indicates that the first small groups of people to settle in Peru were ethnically virtually identical to modern **Amerindians** and filtered into the region from the north around 7000BC. They settled mainly along the coast, attracted by the rich pickings of the Pacific waters, and the sites of their settlements are marked by huge heaps of discarded oyster and mussel shells. By the third millennium BC, more early Peruvians had settled along inland river valleys. Around 1200BC they began to use pottery, and by the 8th century BC they began to cultivate maize and built larger, more impressive settlements.

Among the earliest of these cultures, at **Chavín**, north of Lima, has given its name to an era of burgeoning civilization, with elaborate stone buildings, woven cloth, and richly decorated pottery and gold jewellery.

> ### COCA AND COCAINE
>
> Peru is a major source of the illegal stimulant cocaine, made from the coca leaf. However, under pressure from the USA and its 'war on drugs', cultivation of coca in Peru has fallen. Much of the cocaine base made from the leaf is shipped to neighbouring Colombia for processing into cocaine, while finished cocaine is shipped out from Pacific ports to the international drug market; base and finished cocaine are also moved to Brazil and Bolivia or transhipped to Europe and the USA.

Above: *This Wari pottery figurine is an exhibit in the Pre-Columbian Museum in Cuzco.*

The Chavín culture was succeeded – perhaps as early as the 3rd century BC – by the first civilizations of what is now called the **Classical** period. Cities and small nation-states began to appear in northern Peru, and the people known as the **Mochicas** brought pottery and other arts to a highly sophisticated level, as indicated by the thousands of finds from Mochica tombs. They also built a sophisticated network of canals and aqueducts to irrigate and cultivate arid land. Further south, the **Nazca** civilization created awe-inspiring patterns in the desert sand. In the Andes, the **Wari** culture spread, building citadels at Wari, Pikillakta and Marca Huamachuco.

Around the 10th century AD the Mochica state was replaced by the **Chimu** culture, which remained dominant in the lowlands of northern Peru until the advent of the **Inca**. At around the same time, another culture, the so-called **Tihuanaco** civilization, arose in the Lake Titicaca region, leaving giant stone statues that impressed even the Inca.

The Inca

The rise of the Inca civilization dates from around 1200 AD. The word 'Inca' means 'king' or 'ruler' and the civilization takes its name from its monarchs. The first half-dozen Inca rulers were little more than tribal warrior chieftains, but by the second half of the 14th century the Inca **Yahuar Huacac** had brought the whole Cuzco valley under his sway. His successor, **Viracocha**, consolidated his gains. The defeat of the rival **Chancha** confederation by the Inca **Pachacuti** at the beginning of the 15th century ushered in the golden age of the Inca empire. Pachacuti's successor, **Topa Yupanqui**, conquered all of northern Peru as far as Lima, and his heir **Huayna Capac**, succeeding to the throne in 1493, expanded northward into what is now Ecuador.

HISTORICAL CALENDAR

ca. 7000BC First hunter-gatherers arrive.
3000BC Settlements along the coast, in lowlands and along desert rivers.
1200–200BC Early Horizon period. Key centres are Chavín de Huántar, Caral and Sechin.
200BC–AD600 Intermediate Early Horizon period. Mochica, Tihuanaco and Nazca cultures.
600–900 Middle Horizon period. Wari culture spreads throughout the Andean region.
900–1400 Late Intermediate period. Chimu culture builds Chan Chan near coast. Chachapoyans build Kuélap in Amazonia. Dawn of the Inca Empire.

1400–1532 Late Horizon period. Apogee of the Inca.
1527 Civil war between rival contenders to the Inca throne, Huascar and Atahuallpa.
1531 Arrival of Spanish conquistadors led by Francisco Pizarro.
1532 Pizarro defeats Inca army, murders Atahuallpa. Spanish colonial period begins.
1821 Peru declares independence from Spain.
1824 Spanish troops expelled from Peru.
1836–39 Union with Bolivia, war with Chile. Federation with Bolivia dissolved after defeat by Chile.

1865 Spain finally recognizes Peruvian independence.
1879–84 Nitrate War with Chile ends in defeat for Peru and loss of southern territory.
1962 Leftist APRA government overthrown by military coup.
1980 Return to civilian rule.
1990–2000 Sendero Luminoso terrorists fight against government forces.
2001 President Alberto Fujimori ousted after corruption scandals. Alejandro Toledo Manrique elected president.
2006 Alan García wins presidency.
2007 Earthquake in Pisco and Ica region kills 600.

But Huayna Capac's death in 1527 was followed by a civil war between his sons **Huascar** and **Atahuallpa**. It could not have come at a worse time.

The Spanish Conquest

The Spaniards, who had been expanding their own New World empire for three decades, had already heard of the fabulous wealth of the Inca. From their footholds on the Pacific coast of Darien (modern Panama) the conquistador **Francisco Pizarro** had already made two scouting expeditions to the edge of the Inca domain. In 1531 he made a third expedition to find Atahuallpa on the throne of a weakened empire after defeating his half-brother Huascar. Pizarro's conquistadors, though vastly outnumbered, easily defeated the Inca army, whose soldiers had never encountered armoured horsemen, steel swords, or firearms. Atahuallpa was murdered, the glorious wealth of the Inca treasuries was looted, and by 1533 the Inca empire lay in ruins.

Below: *This bronze statue of the Inca Pachacuti is in Cuzco.*

Opposite: *Peruvian flags in the national colours of red and white fly above a park in the Miraflores district of Lima.*
Below: *A ceremonial bronze shield at the entrance to Cuzco, the capital of the ancient Inca empire.*

Over the next three centuries, Spain imposed **Roman Catholicism** and the **Spanish language**, wiped out most traces of Inca culture, and exploited Peru's mineral wealth. Lima became one of the jewels of the Spanish empire overseas. But the country remained in many ways a backwater. At the beginning of the 19th century, **Napoleon Bonaparte**'s French armies overthrew the Spanish Bourbon dynasty and the South American colonies were left to their own devices. After the end of the Napoleonic Wars (1815) **King Ferdinand VII** of Spain tried to reassert Spanish control, but Peru (like Spain's other colonies) had tasted independence and refused to return to Spanish rule. **Independence** was declared in 1821, and the last Spanish forces were finally defeated at the **Battle of Ayacucho** in 1824 and expelled from Peru. Spain, however, did not formally recognize Peruvian independence until 1865.

Independence and After

Peru's new leaders, a Republican junta, had not planned for the future. Before independence it had been tied to Spain economically as well as politically, but in the 19th century **Britain** and **America** both became interested in Peru's rich mineral resources. British companies invested in mines and built railways to connect them with coastal ports. Peru also became involved in conflicts with its neighbours. In 1836, it joined in a federation with **Bolivia** and went to war with **Chile** – a conflict which ended in victory for Chile, defeat for Peru and Bolivia and the dissolution of the federation in 1839. Bolivia lost its western province and its access to the Pacific to Chile. In a second war with Chile in 1879–84, known as the **Nitrate War**, Peru lost more territory along its southern border, along with its rich nitrate resources.

The 20th Century

Peru remained neutral during both the world wars of the 20th century, and avoided further conflicts at home despite occasional sabre-rattling along its borders. In the 1920s, Peru, Bolivia and Brazil asked Britain for a neutral boundary commission to settle their borders in the Amazon region and a British surveyor, **Colonel Percy Fawcett**, was appointed.

Within Peru, there was growing **economic and political tension** between established land-owners and mine-owners and the increasingly politically aware working class. This was intensified by the fact that most of the country's wealthy ruling class were of European descent, while the country's poorest workers were Quechua, Aymara and mestizo.

Left-leaning political organizations ranged from moderate social democratic parties, through the Communist Party, to even more radical revolutionary groups. For the first half of the century (as in the 19th) power alternated between elected **Liberal** and **Conservative** governments with frequent interludes when the army seized power.

In 1962 the left-leaning **American Popular Revolutionary Alliance** (a moderate socialist party) led by **Dr Victor Raul Haya de la Torre** was elected, only to be overthrown by a military junta led by **General Manuel Perez Godoy**.

Peru returned to democratic leadership in 1980, under the moderate **Fernando Belaunde Terry**, who instituted some measures of social reform. However, the years of dictatorship, coupled with economic problems, created the conditions for the growth of more violent terrorist movements, notably the **Sendero Luminoso** (Shining Path). Modelling their tactics on

PIZARRO AND ATAHUALLPA

The conquistador Francisco Pizarro was – like many of his comrades – an illiterate thug driven by greed for gold. Converting the native peoples of South America to the Catholic faith provided a pretext for plunder. Hearing of the fabulous wealth of the Inca, he made his first expedition down the Pacific coast in 1526, returning in force in 1531. He was at first welcomed by the new Inca ruler, Atahuallpa, whom he promptly kidnapped and – after massacring the Inca army – burned at the stake with the approval of the missionaries who accompanied him.

the Chinese revolutionary leader Mao Zedong, the **Senderistas** waged an extremely violent campaign of terror against the police, the army and the ruling class, first in the remoter parts of the country, then in Lima and other cities. Sendero Luminoso also turned to the cocaine trade to finance its terrorism.

Belaunde was succeeded by the APRA leader **Alan García**. During his term, the Senderistas intensified their attacks and by 1987 more than 11,000 people had been killed.

Elected in 1990, President **Alberto Fujimoro**'s centre-right government turned the economy around and effectively combated Sendero Luminoso. The capture of the Sendero leader **Abimael Guzman** in 2000 ended the Senderistas' 'people's war' and the group disbanded. However, around 200 hard-line combatants remained at large, and after attacks on security forces in December 2005 they threatened to unleash a new wave of violence during the general elections scheduled for April 2006.

However, Fujimoro became increasingly authoritarian and unpopular, and although he was re-elected in 2000 he became involved in a series of corruption scandals and was ousted a year later. **Alejandro Toledo Manrique** was elected president in 2001 with 53.1% of the vote, defeating the centre-left candidate Alan García with 46.9%. Toledo's centrist government has curbed government spending, attempted to decentralize the economy, and has reassured foreign investors, but it too has been plagued by allegations of corruption and like its predecessors has not effectively tackled the problems of poverty and social exclusion.

GOVERNMENT AND ECONOMY
Government

Peru is a **presidential republic**. The president is both head of state and chief of government and is elected by direct vote for a five-year term. The executive branch of government consists of the president, two vice presidents, a prime minister (who does not exercise

---

TUPAC AMARU

Peru's Indian people occasionally revolted against Spanish oppression. The last great Indian rising ended in 1781 with the execution of its leader, **José Gabriel Condorcanqui** (birth date not known), who called himself Inca Tupac Amaru II. Captured in Cuzco, he was torn apart by horses and his limbs were publicly displayed in provincial towns as an example. Legends persisted for years that he had survived and would return to lead another rebellion.

executive power) and a council of ministers appointed by the president.

The country is divided into 24 *departamentos* or **regions** and one **constitutional province** (*provincia constitucional*), Callao. As part of the policy of decentralization, considerable powers are being devolved from central government to the regions, each of which is administered by an elected **regional president** and **regional council**

The executive governs with the advice and consent of the single-chamber **Congress** of 120 members, who are elected every five years by popular vote. Presidential and congressional elections were last held in 2006, with Aprista presidential candidate Alan Garcia winning the presidency in a second-round run-off over the Union por Peru candidate Ollanta Humala Tasso. However, Union por Peru won 45 seats in congress to Aprista's 36. Other main parties elected to congress included the right-wing Unidad Nacional, with 17 seats, and Alianza por el Futuro, with 13. In all, 24 parties contested the congressional elections, but only three won any seats: Frente del Centro, with five seats, and Peru Posible and Restauracion Nacional, with two seats each.

The Economy

Since the dawn of the colonial era in the 16th century, when the conquistadors came in search of precious metals, Peru's economy has been heavily dependent on the **export of raw materials**, including copper, lead, silver, zinc and iron ore. The country is a net exporter of oil, with proven reserves of 408.8 million barrels (enough to make it self-sufficient in oil) and also has substantial natural gas reserves.

Most of Peru's mineral resources are in highland areas, while the coastal waters provide some of the world's richest **fishing** grounds. Coastal ports therefore have a dual role in the Peruvian

MOCHE EROTICA

The Moche culture which dominated Peru around AD200–700 left a remarkable legacy of explicitly sexual art. Prepare to be shocked or aroused by some of the ceramic figures displayed in Peru's superb Museo Larco. Without going into too much detail, many of the figures display Moche men and women indulging in activities that would earn applause at a hard-core porno film festival.

Below: *The changing of the guard outside the Presidential Palace in Lima is a colourful, old-fashioned ceremony.*

PLASTIC POLLUTION

Peru is, sadly, one of the most garbage-strewn countries on the planet. What should be pristine desert is strewn for miles with shreds of discarded blue, green and black plastic bags, and the verges of the Pan-American Highway are one almost continuous rubbish dump of broken glass, cardboard, rusting cans and builder's rubble. Rivers and streams that pass through towns and villages are also choked with trash and often resemble open sewers.

Below: *Loading goods at the docks at Callao, Lima's harbour area and also Peru's most important seaport.*

economy, both as fishing havens and as entrepôts for the export of raw materials from the mines.

The economy is over-dependent on minerals and metals, making Peru very vulnerable to shifts in worldwide commodity prices, currency fluctuations and changes in demand. This over-emphasis on the raw materials sector is reflected in a failure to expand other areas of the economy and infrastructure, which in turn has deterred trade and investment.

The **USA** is, predictably, Peru's biggest trade partner, taking just under 30% of its exports. Less predictably, **China** has become the country's second biggest export market, accounting for 9% of exports and reflecting China's insatiable demand for raw materials. The number three trade partner is **Britain**, reflecting British involvement in the Peruvian economy that dates back to the early 19th century.

After performing poorly for some years, the economy began to recover in 2002. Real GDP growth is now the highest in the region, at more than 6%, and inflation is only 3%.

The Toledo government's fiscal belt-tightening helped to encourage interest from foreign investors after two decades of civil war and repeated economic crises, but better economic performance overall have yet to filter through to the broad mass of the Peruvian people, with 24% of Peruvians classed as living in extreme poverty. **Unemployment** remains relatively high, at around 10% in urban Lima. Elsewhere, true unemployment figures are disguised by seasonal fluctuations and underemployment is a significant problem with 74% classified as underemployed.

Peru's **agricultural sector** is relatively small, account-

Left: *Road transport in much of Peru, especially in the Andes, is slow and old fashioned.*

ing for 8% of gross domestic product and employing around 9% of the workforce. **Industry** – which includes mining and refining of minerals and metals, oil and natural gas production, fishing and fish processing, textiles, clothing, food processing, and steel and other metal industries – accounts for 27% of GDP and employs 18% of the workforce, and the much larger **service sector** – including tourism – employs 73% of Peruvian workers and accounts for an estimated 65% of the country's GDP.

THE PEOPLE

Most of Peru's population live in the towns and cities of the coast, which is home to more than 50% of the country's 28 million people, with almost 73% living in town and cities and fewer than 27% in rural areas. Around 37% of Peru's population is **mestizo** (mixed race, of European and native Amerindian descent). There are two important indigenous Amerindian minorities, the **Quechua** and the **Aymara**, who between them represent some 45% of the total population. The Quechua – the largest indigenous grouping – originally lived in the cultivated valleys of the Andes, at temperate altitudes between 1000m (3000ft) and 3000m (10,000ft) above sea level, and are direct descendants of the Inca culture, while the main Aymara population lives in southern

ENGLISH – QUECHUA	
Good morning • *Allin punchay*	
Good afternoon • *Allin ch'isi*	
Good evening • *Allin tuta*	
Good night • *Pakharinkama*	
Hello • *Allillanchu*	
How are you? • *Imaynallan cashanqui?*	
My name is ... • *Nokan sutiymin ...*	
What is your name? • *Ima sutiyqui?*	
I am from ... • *Nokan kani ...*	
How much? • *Hayk'ataj kay?*	
Thank you • *Yusparasunqui*	
Very delicious • *Sinchi sumaj*	
This is for you • *Kayka kampajmin*	
One more blanket • *Uj frazadatawan*	
Goodbye • *Ripushanin*	
Slowly • *Allillamanta*	
Where is the toilet? • *Maypitaj bano*	
Yes • *Ari*	
No • *Manan*	
Let's go • *Hacu*	

Above: *Island woman from one of Titicaca's floating settlements.*
Opposite: *Football is a major sporting obsession.*

Peru, around Lake Titicaca and the Chilean border region. A relatively small proportion – around 15% – of Peruvians can claim 'pure' **European** descent, but the white minority's political and economic power is great. The percentage of people of **Asian** and **African** descent is even lower, at around 3% (although Lima has a sizeable Chinatown district). Population growth is relatively low, at around 1.36% (2005 estimate).

Of a completely separate culture are the indigenous peoples of **Amazonia**, who comprise 42 identifiable ethnic groups. Like the indigenous peoples of the Brazilian rainforest, their culture and way of life is under relentless pressure from the destruction of the jungle, the encroachment of settlers from outside, disease, and conflict with the economic demands, culture and technology of the 21st century.

Language

Spanish, **Quechua** and **Aymara** are the three official languages of Peru. Most Quechua or Aymara speakers understand and speak Spanish as well. The **literacy** rate is relatively high, at just over 90%.

The Amerindian peoples of Amazonia speak a wide range of **indigenous languages**, belonging to as many as 14 linguistic families, but many of these distinct tongues may be limited to only a few thousand or even a few hundred people, and some languages are at risk of dying out completely.

Religion

The forcible conversion of the conquered peoples of their South American empire to **Roman Catholicism** was considered a sacred duty by the Spaniards and as a result Peru is still overwhelmingly **Christian**, with a little over 80% of the population baptized into the

Catholic church. The state guarantees full religious freedom, but other Christian denominations account for an insignificant 2% of the population. Among the Quechua and Aymara people Catholic Christianity is strongly tinged with older beliefs and rituals, and the indigenous people of the Amazon jungles still retain their own rituals and beliefs of which is little is known to outsiders.

Sport and Recreation

With more than half the population living below the poverty line, many in shanty towns with no proper sports facilities, the most popular sports in Peru are those that require the minimum of expensive equipment.

Peru (like every other South American nation) is crazy about **football**, but has not had as great an impact on global soccer as its rivals, Brazil and Argentina. However, every city or town has its local team and matches are eagerly awaited and watched. **Basketball** is another popular street-level sport.

For better-off, energetic visitors, the country is a paradise for outdoor activities, with some of the world's finest high-altitude **trekking** and challenging **rock climbing** in the Andes, **river rafting** and **kayaking** on Andean watercourses and on the tributaries of the Amazon, and **surfing** on the superb beaches of the far north, near the border with Ecuador.

Music

Archaeologists have found evidence at Peruvian sites of musical instruments some 10,000 years old – many of them little different from traditional instruments that are still played today.

The best known (if not the best loved) of Peruvian native instruments is the **pan-pipe**, a multi-fluted wind instrument made from reeds from the Titicaca region, and itinerant Peruvian pan-pipe bands can be heard not only in the streets of Lima but in cities such as Madrid, Barcelona, Berlin, London and around the world.

ENGLISH – SPANISH
Good morning • *Buenos días*
Good afternoon • *Buenas tardes*
Good evening/good night • *Buenas noches*
Hello • *Hola*
How are you? • *¿Cómo está usted?*
My name is • *Mi nombre es*
What is your name? • *¿Cómo te llamas?*
I am from … • *Yo soy de …*
How much? • *¿Cuánto cuesta?*
Thank you • *Gracias*
Very delicious • *Muy deliciosa*
This is for you • *Esto es para ti*
One more blanket • *Una frazada más*
Goodbye • *Adios*
Slowly • *Lento*
Where is the toilet? • *¿Dónde está el baño?*
Yes/No • *Si/No*
Let's go • *Vamos*

PISCO

Peru's native drink is pisco, a clear, fiery brandy distilled from Peruvian varieties of grape and best drunk in a pisco sour, the national cocktail. The country also has an expanding wine industry, a legacy both of the Spanish era and of modern wine-growing techniques which have led to a great improvement in the quality of Peruvian-made wines in the last decade.

Above: *Traditional dancers perform for local and tourist audiences in Cuzco, but folk dancing is still alive and kicking.*
Below: *Pisco, distilled from grape skins, is Peru's powerful national spirit.*

Two typically Peruvian rhythms, the *huayno* and the *marinera*, form the basis of much Peruvian music, while in Lima and the north coast, where most of Peru's people of African descent live, **percussion** instruments such as the *cajon* and the *quijada de burro* influence local rhythms. In the Amazon region, wooden drums such as the *manguare* have traditionally been used not only to make music but also to relay messages over vast distances.

Despite its deep traditional roots, Peruvian music is as open to world influences as any musical culture in the 21st century, creating new musical strands such as *chicha*, the music of the Lima streets, and a distinctively Peruvian style of jazz that blends modern and African-American elements with Spanish and indigenous influences, pioneered by bands such as **Perujazz** (Pierre Magnet, Luis Solar, Manongo Mujica and Noel Marambio). Leading contemporary Afro-Peruvian musicians include the singer **Eva Ayllon**. **Lorenzo Palacios**, nicknamed 'Chacalon' is the current king of *chicha* and Peru's homeground brand of indie rock has been represented for some 20 years by 'underground' band **Leusemia**.

Art and Architecture

The artistic and architectural achievements of the

ancient indigenous peoples of Peru almost defy belief, ranging from the largest mud-brick city in the ancient world to the cyclopean stone walls of Cuzco, Machu Picchu and Kuélap and the golden glories of the Sipán tombs – all carried out without metal implements.

Above: Grandiose, grimy and crumbling colonial and Republican-era buildings dominate the streets of downtown Lima.

The **Spanish colonial** era, between 1532 and 1821, also endowed Peru with a collection of gorgeously grandiose religious buildings, such as the magnificent Convent of Santo Domingo, in Cuzco, and the Convent of Santa Catalina in the 'white city' of Arequipa, where there are also a number of fine Baroque buildings dating from the colonial era.

In Cuzco, a unique **mestizo style** of art and architecture developed after the Conquest, combining a native Quechua eye for brilliant colour with Catholic subjects and themes and exemplified by the decoration of the Compañía de Jesús church and Cuzco Cathedral. Hand-painted copies imitating the themes of this early 'Cuzco School' of painting are much in demand today.

A rich **vernacular artistic tradition** also pervades Peru. Handloom-woven textiles (cotton, llama and alpaca wool), pottery, and heavy silver jewellery are made in Cuzco's San Blas quarter by long-established family workshops, notably those of the Mendivil, La Torre, Olave, and Merida families.

FERNANDO DE SZYSZLO VALDELOMAR

Fernando de Szyszlo Valdelomar (b. 1925) is Peru's most important modern painter. He draws his inspiration from the landscapes of his native Lima, the ocean and the coastal deserts in abstract works such as *Anabase* (1982), *Abolition of Death* (1987) and *Black Sun* (1992), and works mainly in acrylic on fabric. Trained as an architect, he studied painting at the School of Art in Lima's Catholic University.

Above: *Llama, alpaca and sheep's wool are traditionally woven into brilliantly coloured and patterned textiles. The best examples of this traditional craft command high prices.*

FLORA TRISTAN

Notable authors and poets of 19th-century Peru include Flora Tristan (1803–44). The daughter of an exiled Spanish-Peruvian father and a French mother, she grew up in poverty in France. Travelling to Peru in 1833 to seek her inheritance, she lived with her father's wealthy relatives in Arequipa but – raised in revolutionary France – also perceived great social injustice, which formed the theme of *Pilgrimages of an Outcast*, published in 1837 in France.

Literature

Peru's literary tradition is not strong. The Inca society was pre-literate, and all forms of expression under Spanish rule were strictly constrained.

Dictatorships and reactionary governments through the 19th and 20th centuries also discouraged free literary development.

Lima-born **Cesar Moro** (1903–56) is probably Peru's most famous poet and is considered to be one of South America's most important surrealist poets. Other national literary figures who are less well known outside Peru include the authors and essayists **Javier Perez de Cuellar** and **Fernando Savater**.

Peru's most respected contemporary literary figure is the author **Mario Vargas Llosa**, born in Arequipa in 1936. Vargas Llosa's novels, such as *La Fiesta del Chivo* (*The Feast of the Goat*) (2000), are mainly political polemics, and the author has been criticizing corruption and tyranny in South American society for some 40 years. Vargas Llosa became actively involved in Peruvian politics when he ran for president in 1990, but was defeated. In 1993 he took Spanish citizenship.

Food and Drink

Peru's multicultural heritage and hugely varied geography and climate contribute to an equally varied national menu.

Seafood is excellent in Lima and along the coast, where dishes such as *cebiche* (chunks of raw fish marinated in lime juice, chopped onion and chilli peppers), *escabeche* (fried fish marinated in vinegar and steamed with onion) and *parihuella* (a rich seafood and shellfish broth) are popular. Also on the menu are **main dishes**

such as *causa limena relena* (mashed sweet potatoes seasoned with pepper and lime and stuffed with tuna or chicken), *lomo saltado* (sliced beef with onion, tomato and potato) and *aji de gallina* (diced chicken in a thick cream and cheese sauce seasoned with peppers and nuts and served with rice).

Dessert dishes include *mazamorra morada*, a sweet jelly made from purple maize and stewed with fruit; *suspiro a la limena*, meringue with vanilla cream; and *picarones*, small sweet doughnuts made from sweet potato and squash and sweetened with carob syrup.

In Cuzco, **local delicacies** include *lawa*, a soup made from maize and beans; *chicharron con mote*, pork fritters with fresh maize; and *chiriuchu*, roast guinea pig or chicken with a pancake of corn flour filled with cheese, dried meat and peppers. Near Lake Titicaca, you may encounter *sopa chairo*, a beef and lamb soup with potatoes, beans, squash, cabbage and chilli, or steaks of alpaca, which are similar to venison.

In the Cordillera Huayhuash region of the Andes, traditional dishes range from stewed guinea pig in spicy sauce (*picante de cuy*) to roast suckling pig, llama jerky known as *charqui*, sheep's-head soup with tripe (*pecan caldo*) and *pachamanca*, meat, potatoes and young maize cooked underground over hot stones.

COCKTAIL HOUR

For a typically Peruvian cocktail, try one of these:

Pisco Sour
3 oz (90ml) pisco
1 oz (30ml) lemon juice
1 oz (30ml) sugar syrup (or 2 tablespoons sugar)
1 egg white
4 ice cubes, thoroughly crushed
1 drop Angostura bitters

Algarrobina
1½ oz (45ml) pisco
1 teaspoon sugar
½ oz (15ml) honey
2 oz (60ml) condensed milk
1 egg yolk
4 ice cubes, crushed
powdered cinnamon

Capitan
2 oz (60ml) sweet vermouth
1½ oz (45ml) pisco
4 ice cubes
Shake and serve.

Left: Cuy al horno *(roast guinea pig) is a popular dish throughout Peru, but some visitors find its appearance a bit disturbing.*

2
Lima and Callao

Peru's capital lies on the Pacific coast, approximately halfway between the country's northern border with Ecuador and its southern border with Chile.

The **Lima** conurbation has almost doubled in size and population in the last 25 years, and has merged with the port area of **Callao** which was originally a separate city.

With a population estimated at almost seven million people, Lima is the home of almost one in four Peruvians and is the base for two thirds of the country's **commerce** and **industry**.

The outskirts of Lima are an unwelcoming mix of prosaic modern residential suburbs, industrial grime and squalid shanty towns, but the historic heart of the city conceals a treasury of **colonial architecture** which has earned it UNESCO World Heritage Site status, a trace of the 1950s glamour that attracted film stars and celebrities such as John Wayne (who married a Lima socialite, Maria del Pilar Pallete), Orson Welles and Ava Gardner to the **Gran Hotel Bolivar**, which in its heyday was the most luxurious in South America.

Although the valley of the **Rimac River** has been inhabited for more than 1000 years, modern Lima was founded in 1535 by the conquistador **Francisco Pizarro**, who was attracted by its strategic location and good anchorage at nearby Callao. It grew to be the most important city in Spain's overseas empire, a port of call for ships plying between the other Pacific coast colonies and for merchant ships and whaling vessels

---

DON'T MISS

*** Plaza San Martín:** the heart of historic Lima.
*** Cathedral:** grandiose example of South American religious architecture.
*** Church of San Francisco:** gracious colonial buildings.
*** Museo de la Nación (Museum of the Nations):** fine collection of exhibits spanning a rich national history.

Opposite: *The front door of the Casa Aliaga, one of Lima's surviving gracious colonial mansions.*

Above: *The severe Baroque façade of Lima Cathedral disguises a magnificent interior.*

STREET CRIME

Lima is no longer as outright dangerous as it was during the Senderista terrorist era but street crime is rife and bag-snatchers and pickpockets are active even in the smartest suburbs. Carry cash and credit cards in a concealed money belt, not a handbag. Do not carry your camera round your neck and do not accept the offer of a drink from a stranger – tourists have been drugged, then robbed.

from the United States and Britain. During the early 20th century, Lima enjoyed a reputation as the most modern and exciting city in South America, and there are echoes of this *belle époque* in the grand houses of some of its older residential suburbs.

The opening of the **Panama Canal** in 1914, allowing ships to travel from the Caribbean to the Pacific without rounding the tip of South America, somewhat reduced its importance as a seaport, but it remains by far Peru's biggest and most vibrant city. Away from the centre, **Miraflores** is the city's gleaming modern shopping and upscale entertainment area. **San Isidro** is the main business and financial district but also has parks, hotels, and expensive residential areas, along with the **Lima Golf Club**, one of the largest green areas in the capital. **Barranco**, south of Miraflores on the coast, is the capital's most bohemian quarter and is packed with bars and music venues.

One of Lima's biggest attractions is **food**. The city has earned a reputation as the gastronomic capital of South America with great Pacific seafood, vegetables from the Andes and tropical fruits from the Amazon, all prepared in combinations unique to Peru.

Many visitors waste no time in Peru's ramshackle capital, preferring to head straight for the Inca Trail, Lake Titicaca or the Amazon, but the city has its attractions and two to three days here is time well spent.

Lima is also Peru's **shopping** capital. Anything that can be found in the tourist spots of the Andes can also be found here – and often at prices that compare favourably with those in Cuzco or Arequipa. Colourful textiles, heavy traditional silver jewellery, wood carvings, paintings in the style of the Cuzco School,

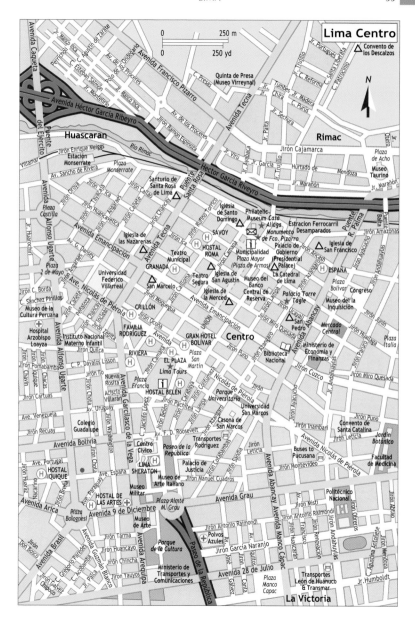

Lima Centro

△ Convento de
los Descalzos

Above: The Archbishop's Palace is located on the Plaza de Armas.

colonial antiques and pre-Conquest treasures can all be found in Peru's antique shops and markets. The main handicraft markets are in Miraflores (Av Petit Thouars, blocks 48–52), in the city centre at Conde de Superunda and Carabaya, and in the Pueblo Libre district at Av La Marina, blocks 6–8.

PLAZA MAYOR (PLAZA DE ARMAS)

The Plaza Mayor, the city's main square, is the heart of historic Lima. This is where Pizarro founded the city, and where Peruvians declared their independence from Spain in 1821. Its centrepiece is a graceful bronze **fountain** dating from 1650, and the square is surrounded by grandiose buildings, with the **Cathedral** and the **Archbishop's Palace** on the east side, the **Presidential Palace** with its ceremonial guards in fancy uniforms on the north, and the **City Hall** on the west side.

Lima Cathedral ★★★

The Cathedral's severe Baroque façade belies a magnificent interior which glitters with gold leaf and superbly carved altars and choir stalls. Every inch of woodwork seems to be carved or painted, and paintings and statues dating from the 17th and 18th centuries adorn the walls. Built in 1625, the Cathedral was extensively rebuilt after being damaged by a series of earthquakes in 1687, 1746 and most severely in 1940. The Cathedral also contains the tomb of the conquistador Francisco Pizarro. Open Monday–Friday 09:00–16:30 and Saturday 10:00–16:30.

Palacio de Gobierno (Presidential Palace) ★

Built in 1937, this pompous pile is the residence of Peru's head of state and is guarded by soldiers in colourful uniforms that date back to the 19th century.

LIMA'S LAST RESERVE

Between Lima and the beaches (18km/11 miles south of Lima), the **Pantanos de Villa** wetlands (access by car from Avenida Huaylas) cover almost 400ha (990 acres) of marsh and reed bed, providing a haven for more than 150 resident and migrant bird species. The reserve boasts 178 bird species, of which 77 are migratory, including the great grebe, the pied-billed grebe, the snowy egret, the black-crowned night heron, the cinnamon teal, the osprey, the common moorhen, the American coot, the sanderling, the greater yellowlegs and the gray gull.

Their rifles, however, are noticeably more up to date. A statue of Francisco Pizarro stands outside. Guided tours take place daily; book 48 hours ahead at the Palace Public Relations Office, Jirón de la Uonin, Plaza Pizarro, tel: 311 3908. The ceremonial changing of the Palace Guard is at 12:00 daily.

Iglesia de San Francisco (Church of St Francis) ★★★

At the corner of Ancash and Lampa, this complex of lovely colonial buildings includes the Church and Convent of San Francisco, the Soledad Chapel and the Milagro Chapel. The 17th-century cloisters are graced by blue tiles (*azulejos*) imported from Seville. Within, the **Museum of Religious Art** has some fine statues and altarpieces, and beneath is an eerie complex of tunnels and catacombs. Open daily 09:00–18:00.

Museo de la Nación ★★★

A visit to this well-designed museum with its wonderful collection of pre-Conquest works of art, sculptures, pottery and textiles from all over Peru – representing virtually every era and culture – is essential for an understanding of the country's history and the complex roots of its present-day culture. Models of the most important of Peru's ancient ruined cities and temples also help the visitor to acquire a broader perspective. At Javier Prado Este 2466, it is open 09:00–17:00 Tuesday–Sunday

Iglesia de Santo Domingo ★★

Begun in 1535, this church was not completed until the end of the following century. Its most striking features are the soaring dome, the collection of Baroque religious sculptures in the chapel, and the finely carved cedarwood choirs. The church is at the corner of Camaná and Superunda and is open 09:00–12:30 and 15:00–18:00 Monday–Saturday and 09:00–13:00 Sunday.

FROST IN THE JUNGLE?

Peru is one of the countries most vulnerable to extreme weather fluctuations. Floods are a perennial problem, especially in the tropical north. More than 20 people were killed by flooding in January 2008, and thousands more were made homeless. And the changing global climate is likely to inflict more extreme weather phenomena in coming years, say weather scientists – including even the possibility of the jungle frosts that have been reported from other tropical rainforest regions.

Below: *The interior of San Francisco Monastery.*

Santuario de Santa Rosa de Lima *

Named for South America's first Catholic saint, and claimed to be built next to her birthplace, the church encloses an unassuming adobe chapel where St Rose of Lima prayed and meditated. It is open daily 09:00–12:30 and 17:00–18:30.

Iglesia de las Nazarenas *

Built on a site incorporating a 17th-century fresco painted by one of the freed slaves who once lived in this part of Lima and which miraculously survived the 1655 earthquake, this 18th-century church is the scene of some of Lima's most colourful religious processions. One of the most important takes place on 18 October each year, when a copy of the fresco is paraded around the streets. The church is located at the corner of Huancavelica and Tacna and is open 07:00–12:00 and 17:00–20:30 Monday–Saturday and 06:30–13:00 and 17:00–20:30 Sunday.

Iglesia de la Merced *

This 18th-century church, situated at the corner of Jirón de la Union and Miró Quesada, is one of Lima's finest,

Opposite: *The balcony of the Palacio Torre Tagle, former home of the treasurer of the Spanish Royal Fleet, fronts one of the country's finest examples of colonial architecture.*
Right: *Paseo de Aguas in the Rimac district of Lima.*

with a façade in the Churriguerra style
(*see* panel, page 38), a fine collection of
works of art from the colonial era, including statues and portraits in oils of
colonial grandees, and also a beautiful
tiled sacristy. It is open 08:00–12:00 and
16:00–20:00 daily.

Rimac *

Spanish influence is very evident in the
old-fashioned streets of the Rimac district,
located across the Rimac River from the
old city centre and connected to it by a
series of old bridges.

Rimac has some of Lima's best traditional music clubs and restaurants, and in
the centre of its narrow streets and
squares is the **Plaza de Acho**, one of the
oldest bullrings outside Spain. Built in
1768, it comes into its own every year in
October when it hosts the annual **Señor
de Los Milagros** (Our Lord of the Miracles) season of
corridas. Bulls and toreadors are celebrated in the
Museo Taurino, on the bullfight plaza at Huaylgayoc
332, with displays of fancy costumes and gaudy bullfight posters.

Palacio Torre Tagle *

This grand building, with its ornate façade, carved
wooden balconies and Baroque stone doorway, was
the home of the **Marquis of Torre Tagle**, treasurer of the
Spanish Royal Fleet, and was built for him in 1730.
One of the country's most dazzling examples of colonial architecture, the interior of the palace has
wonderful features such as blue tiles from Seville,
soaring coffered ceilings and Moorish-style arches. It is
now occupied by the Peruvian Foreign Ministry and is
not normally open to the public, except by special
arrangement (contact the Cultural Office, tel: 311 2400,
for a guided tour).

SANTA ROSA DE LIMA

Isabel Flores de Oliva (1586–
1617) is the patroness of the
Americas and the first person
to be canonized on the con-
tinent. Born in Lima, she
took the name Rose at her
confirmation and set out on
a life of fasting, prayer, self-
mortification and charity.
She died at the age of 31
(her health almost certainly
ruined by her lifestyle, which
included resting on a bed of
broken glass, stones, and
thorns. She was beatified by
Pope Clement IX, in 1667,
and canonized in 1671 by
Clement X.

CHURRIGUERESQUE STYLE

Though born in Spain, the Churrigueresque style of religious architecture reached its finest flowering in colonial Mexico and Peru, where disciples of Jose Benito Churriguera (1665–1725) built dozens of striking churches and cathedrals in the distinctive, elaborate style of high Baroque that was developed in Madrid and Barcelona by Churriguera, his brothers, sons and nephews. Churriguera's fascination with exuberant detail, which clashes strikingly with the severity of contemporary Spanish Renaissance buildings, seems to have struck a chord in Peru – perhaps it reminded the recently converted native Peruvian people of the equally elaborate friezes and murals of their ancient temples.

LIMA FESTIVALS

October is the month-long festival of Nuestro Señor de Los Milagros (Our Lord of the Miracles), when a replica of the supposedly miraculous fresco from the Church of Las Nazarenas (see page 36) in the Pachacamilla district is paraded through the streets on a silver litter, followed by thousands of people. October is also bullfight season, with gory spectacles taking place in the historic Plaza de Acho bullring (see page 37).

Museo de la Inquisición ★

The Inquisition's reign of religious fanaticism lasted longer in the Spanish colonies than in Europe, ending only with independence, when the Inquisition ceased to be the propaganda wing of the Spanish Empire. The museum building was the Inquisition's Peruvian headquarters from 1570 until 1820, and its torture rooms – complete with creepy life-size waxworks – can be seen on a guided tour. Located at Jirón Junín 548, it is open 09:00–17:00 daily, with tours every 30 minutes.

Plaza San Martín ★★

This grand square was laid out in the early years of the 20th century, when Lima still had pretensions to being the most important city in South America. Taking its inspiration from French *belle époque* urban design, it is dominated by an **equestrian statue**, in bronze, of **General San Martín**, who led the fight for independence from Spain, erected in 1921 on the centenary of the Peruvian Republic. A second grand statue is Peru's equivalent of New York's Statue of Liberty – the **Madre Patria** (Mother of the Fatherland). On one side of the square is Peru's grandest hotel, the **Gran Hotel Bolivar** (named after Simon Bolivar, the 'George Washington of South America'), where such celebrities as John Wayne and Orson Welles sipped pisco sours in the 1930s.

Parque de la Cultura and Museo de Arte **

The Museo de Arte is Peru's national museum of fine arts, with a collection of paintings and sculpture spanning the four centuries of colonial rule as well as relics from the pre-Colonial era. The surrounding park, with its oriental garden and open-air amphitheatre, was refurbished in the 1990s and offers a welcome escape from the hurly-burly of Lima street life. At Paseo de Colon 125, it is open 10:00–17:00 Thu–Tue, closed Wed.

Museo de Oro del Perú **

There have been allegations that many of the exhibits in this private collection (in the Monterrico district east of the centre) are cunning fakes, but they are still glitteringly spectacular, ranging from cloaks and headdresses adorned with solid gold to huge earrings. The building also houses an eccentric arms museum, stuffed with lethal weaponry spanning several centuries, from medieval arquebuses to 19th-century muzzle-loaders. Alonso de Molina 1100, open daily 11:30–19:00.

Casa Aliaga *

As old as Lima itself, this lavish colonial mansion was founded by one of Pizarro's conquistadors, **Jeronimo de Aliaga**, who had it built on top of the ruins of a much earlier temple, using the stones of the building for his foundations. Expanded and embellished over the centuries, it is still inhabited by his descendants, who

> **BUYING DRUGS**
>
> You will almost certainly be offered cocaine by dealers on the streets of Lima, Cuzco and other cities. Be aware that – quite apart from the health risks involved in cocaine use – many dealers are also informers, turning in unwary gringos to the police. Cocaine is omnipresent in Peru, but is also illegal, as it is elsewhere, and penalties for possession are severe.

Opposite: *Life-size wax figures of Inquisitors in the Museum of the Inquisition, Lima, commemorate a dark era of intolerance.*
Below: *The elegant and lavishly furnished and decorated dining room of the Casa Aliaga.*

JULIO RAMON RIBEYRO

Julio Ramon Ribeyro (1929–94) is the storyteller of Lima's dark side. His characters are the marginalized people of the city and of Peru, doomed by their environment and their own flaws to remain on the outskirts of society. Ribeyro's Lima is a city dominated by injustice, violence and poverty. Ribeyro won recognition as one of South America's literary talents shortly before his death in 1994.

allow its impressive public rooms and salons to be used as venues for various prestigious cultural events. With its huge, luxurious chambers surrounding a beautiful inner patio, it is typical of the great colonial mansions built by the wealthy oligarchs of Peru. At Jirón de la Union 224, visits are by appointment only, tel: 424 5110.

Museo Nacional de Antropologia, Arqueologia y Historia *

The Museum of Anthropology, Archeology and History houses an eclectic collection of finds from all Peru's most important archaeological sites, as well as colonial furniture and paintings. At Plaza Bolivar, it is open Tue–Sat 09:00–17:00, Sun 09:00–16:00, closed Mon.

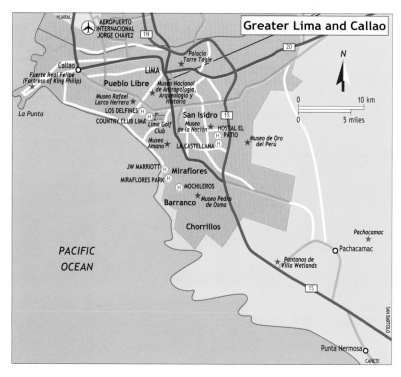

Museo Rafael Larco Herrera *

This museum in the Pueblo Libre district next to San Isidro (named after a former vice president) houses a remarkable collection of pre-Columbian ceramics and gold and silver objects, including some startling erotic sculpture. Open daily 09:00–18:00.

MIRAFLORES

High-rise hotels and modern apartment blocks dominate the blue water and sandy beaches of Lima's seaside suburb. Miraflores is one of Lima's most modern and attractive districts for the visitor, with luxury hotels, excellent international restaurants, upscale shopping malls, art galleries and craft shops, especially along Avenida Petit Thouars. It also has good beaches for surfing, and the cliffs along its coast are popular with hang-gliders.

Museo Amano *

This museum has a fine collection of pre-Conquest pottery. At Retiro 160, it is open 09:00–18:00 daily.

BARRANCO

The Barranco district, south of Miraflores behind the coastal strip known as the Costa Verde or 'green coast', was the favourite beach resort and residential area for well-off city-dwellers in the first part of the 20th century, then went through several decades of seedy decline. Since the 1990s it has been making a comeback, and the gracious old post-Colonial mansions along its tree-lined streets are once more in demand. In summer, there are often open-air concerts and performances in Barranco's parks and public gardens. The district is popular with

Above: *With its colonial buildings, flower-filled parks, broad streets and modern shops and restaurants, Miraflores is the wealthiest and most attractive part of Lima.*

Above: Picarones, *sold from street vendors' stalls like this one in Miraflores, are a favourite Peruvian snack.*

artists and musicians of all kinds and has some good bars and cafés.

Museo Pedro de Osma ★
This is a private museum housed in a grand old mansion and displaying some fine relics of the colonial era, including furniture, silver and sculpture. San Pedro de Osma 423, open 10:00–13:30 and 14:30–18:00 Thu–Sun.

Chorrillos

Merging with Barranco to the north, Chorrillos is famous for its seafood restaurants and snack bars called *picanterías* (similar to Spanish tapas bars) and its streets, like Barranco's, are lined with dignified old mansions built in the post-Independence years of the 19th century. From the top of the Morro Solar hill in the centre of Chorrillos there are fine views of the coast, the island of Isla San Lorenzo just offshore, and Callao.

Callao and La Punta

Urban sprawl connects Lima with Callao, 14km (9 miles) west of the city centre. **Callao**, founded in 1537 as the port of Lima, was originally a separate community and is today a separate administrative region. It is still Peru's largest port and retains a distinctly raffish seaport character, and wandering around its scruffy streets alone is inadvisable, as street crime is very common. Callao's only historic sight is the stolid **Fuerte Real Felipe** (Fortress of King Philip), with its five-sided ramparts (at Plaza Independencia, it is open daily 09:00–14:00, for guided visits only). The **Punta Peninsula**, sheltering the harbour from the Pacific

---

Lima Nightlife

Lima's tourist hotels put on folklore shows, but for more authentic nightlife head for one of the city's hundreds of *peñas* and their *criolla* music. *Criolla* music blends African, Hispanic and Amerindian influences in romantic ballads and waltzes, and sometimes crosses over into jazz as well. The Barranco district is full of *peñas*; most charge a cover price, open around 22:00, and stay open until the early hours.

breakers, is off limits to visitors as it is the headquarters of the Peruvian Navy.

South of the City **

To get away from the city in summer, Lima folk head south down the Pan-American Highway to a 100km (65-mile) string of sandy and pebbly beaches that begins around 35km (21 miles) south of the city centre and stretches south all the way to Cañete.

The main resort areas along this coast include **La Qebrada**, **Santa María**, **Punta Hermosa** and **San Bartolo**, with hotels, restaurants and nightlife catering mainly to Peruvian holiday-makers. **Señoritas**, **Penascal**, **Pico Alta** and **Punta Rocas** beaches have good surf, while **Chepeconde**, **Gallardo** and **Cerro Colorado** are undeveloped, with camp sites that are popular with young budget travellers from Lima.

Pachacamac **

First excavated in the late 19th century, this huge complex of mud-brick ramparts, temples and pyramids in a semi-desert landscape 32km (20 miles) south of Lima bears traces of the Huari and Inca cultures as well as its original Pachacamac builders. In 2005, archaeologists discovered a multilevel grave site containing the remains of up to 100 mummified Inca and pre-Inca bodies, and excavation on the site continues. Open 09:00–17:00 Mon–Fri. There is an admission charge.

> **VILLA EL SALVADOR**
>
> On the outskirts of Lima, the former shantytown of Villa El Salvador is a rare community success story. In 1971, nearly 200 families from the inner-city slums occupied a tract of desert and were soon joined by thousands more. After clashes between troops and squatters, the government offered the families a massive plot of desert at Tablada de Lurin, 25km (16 miles) south of the city. Nearly 7000 families settled in the dunes, and Villa El Salvador was born. Its founders drew up plans for expansion and set aside land for farming, industry, schools, clinics and parks. Today, Villa El Salvador is a vibrant commercial and residential area, and a model for similar experiments in self-sufficiency worldwide.

Left: *San Bartolo is a popular beach resort for Peruvians.*

Lima and Callao at a Glance

Oct–Apr is the dry, sunny season. Heavy rain and cold weather are unusual, but the weather in Lima is cool, damp and overcast from May to Oct, with frequent sea mists.

Direct **flights** from European cities including Madrid and Amsterdam. Spanish airline Iberia has the most flights and cheapest fares from Europe. There are also direct flights to most South American capitals and to Miami, Los Angeles and New York in the USA with American Airlines and Continental Airlines. The main airline for flights within Peru is AeroCondor (tel: 0800 00600, www.aerocondor.com.pe) with a network that includes Lima, Arequipa, Ayacucho, Cuzco, Cajamarca, Ica, Iquitos, Juliaca, Nasca, Piura, Puerto Maldonado, Pacallpa, Tacna, Trujillo and Tumes. Chilean-owned LAN (www.lan.com) flies three times daily between Lima and Cusco, three times daily between Lima and Arequipa, twice daily between Arequipa and Juliaca (for Lake Titicaca) and daily between Cusco and Puerto Maldonada. TACA (www.taca.com) flies daily between Lima and Cusco. **Buses** run on the Pan-American Highway to Tumbes on the Ecuador border (1370km north) and Tacna on the Chilean border (1291km south) and all points between. Buses also

run to Cuzco and other inland cities. Main companies are Cruz del Sur (Quilca 531, tel: 424 1005, www.cruzdelsur. com) and Ormeno (Carlos Zavala Loayza 177, tel: 427 5679, www.ascinsa.com). Both operate luxury coaches as well as standard services. **Trains** connect Lima with Huancayo, 3260m (10,800ft) above sea level, reaching 4781m (15,500ft) above sea level on the way. This is a spectacular journey but departures are irregular; contact Desamparados Railway Station, Ancash 201, tel: 361 2828.

Unlicensed **cabs** compete with licensed yellow **taxis**; agree a fare before getting in. If travelling alone, do not use unlicenced cabs. Local **buses** (micros) and **minibuses** (combis) are cheap but unbelievably crowded and there is a high incidence of pickpocketing and bag-snatching. Urbanito **buses** connect the airport with hotels in the centre and Miraflores. **Shared taxis** (taxis colectivos) run on fixed routes on the main avenues, between central Lima and Miraflores, and to the airport and Callao. Fares are very cheap and you can board or get off at any point along the way.

LUXURY
Lima Sheraton Hotel and Casino, tel: 315 5022, www.

sheraton.com In the historic centre of Lima with 431 rooms including 85 luxury tower rooms and suites. There are live folklore shows in the fine Las Palmeras restaurant and a shuttle service to the Miraflores district.
Miraflores Park Hotel, Av. Malecon de la Reserva 1035, Miraflores, tel: 242 3000, www.mirapark.com Luxurious modern hotel with fine views and impeccable service in Lima's posh seaside district.
Los Delfines Summit Hotel and Casino, Los Eucaliptos 555, San Isidro, tel: 215 7000, www.losdelfines.com Splendid modern hotel with views of San Isidro Golf Course, indoor and outdoor pools, business centre, three bars and restaurants and secure parking.
JW Marriott Hotel and Stellaris Casino, Malecon de la Reserva 615, Miraflores, tel: 217 7000, www.marriott.com All 300 rooms at this fine hotel have ocean views and facilities are excellent.
Country Club Lima Hotel, Los Eucaliptos 590, San Isidro, tel: 611 9000, www.hotel country.com Reopened as one of the finest places to stay in the capital, with grand public areas and bedrooms and modern facilities including pool and gym.

MID-RANGE
Gran Hotel Bolivar, Jirón de la Union 958, tel: 428 7672, e-mail: bolivar@terra.com.pe

Lima and Callao at a Glance

The bedrooms and corridors could do with a lick of paint – and new plumbing – but the grand bar is still the place to revel in nostalgia over a pisco sour. Rates are affordable and the location central.

Casa Andina Miraflores, Av. 28 de Julio 1088, Miraflores, tel: 241 4050, www.casa-andina.com This colourful and affordable hotel offers the best value for money in Miraflores, with comfortable rooms and adequate facilities.

Hostal el Patio, Diez Canseco 341A, Miraflores, tel: 444 2107, www.hostalpatio.net With 21 rooms including 8 suites, this small, friendly hotel is near the centre of Miraflores and has a pretty patio.

BUDGET
Hotel La Castellana, Miraflores, tel: 444 4662, www.hotel-la-castellana.com Comfortable; surprisingly good value for money in the expensive Miraflores district.

Hostal Mochileros, Barranco, tel: 247 8643, www.back packersperu.com In Barranco; offers cheap rooms with a bit of character.

Hotel España, Azarango 105, tel: 428 5546, www.hotel espanaperu.com A colourful, characterful, central place to stay, near the Plaza de Armas. It has a roof-garden, café bar, and beds in dormitory rooms, singles and doubles with or without private bathroom. It is very cheap.

Hostal Mami Panchita, Av. Federico Gallesi 198, tel: 263 7203, www.mami panchita. com Dutch-owned three-star guesthouse with 14 rooms, between Miraflores and the historic centre, with its own in-house travel agency.

LUXURY
El Señorio del Sulco, Malecon Cisneros 1470, Miraflores, tel: 441 0389. A Lima landmark which serves all the best Peruvian regional dishes, embellished by great pisco sours and views of the Pacific.

Benihana, Jockey Plaza Shopping Centre, tel: 435 1777. High-class Italian restaurant in one of the city's smart shopping malls.

Haiti, Avenida Diagonal 160, tel: 445 0539. Adventurous contemporary fusion cooking with Pacific, Caribbean and South American influences.

MID-RANGE
Pescados Capitales, Av. La Mar 1337, Miraflores, tel: 421 8808. This seafood restaurant serves the best *ceviche* in town.

Restaurant Puntarenas, Jirón Santa Teresa 455, Chorrillos, tel: 467 0053. Not city centre but worth the journey for excellent Peruvian specialties.

BUDGET
Wa Lok, Paruro 864, Bario Chino, tel: 427 2656. In Lima's Chinatown; noodle dishes and dim sum are cheap and filling.

Puerto Escondido, Avenida Huaylas Cuadra 14, tel: 252 1883. This seafood restaurant is very good value for money and the fish is excellent.

Aracari Tours, Av. Pardo 610, Miraflores, tel: (01) 242 6673, www.aracari.com 4–8-day itineraries throughout Peru, including trips to Cuzco and the Sacred Valley, Machu Picchu, Nazca, Huascarán, Kuélap, Arequipa, the north, and Titicaca; also trekking, riding and rafting adventures.

PromPeru (Commission for the Promotion of Peru), Cale Uno Oeste 050, San Isidro, Lima, tel: 224 3131, www.peru.org.pe

LIMA	J	F	M	A	M	J	J	A	S	O	N	D
AVERAGE TEMP. °F	82	83	83	80	74	68	67	66	68	71	74	78
AVERAGE TEMP. °C	28	28	28	27	23	20	19	19	20	22	23	26
RAINFALL in	0.1	0	0	0	0.2	0.2	0.3	0.3	0.3	0.1	0.1	0
RAINFALL mm	3	0	0	0	5	5	8	8	8	3	3	0
DAYS OF RAINFALL	0.5	0.1	0.1	0.2	0.8	1	1	2	1	0.2	0.2	0.1

3. Cuzco, the Inca Trail and Machu Picchu

Cuzco is beyond doubt the biggest single tourism magnet in Peru and one of the most famous historic sites in the world, blending a unique and stunning pre-Columbian heritage with a dazzling colonial legacy and set among some of the most spectacular scenery on the planet.

Little wonder, then, that of the hundreds of thousands who visit each year, most make their way straight here, to the beginning of the legendary **Inca Trail**.

Once the capital of the Inca (and other empires before them), Cuzco's name in Quechua means 'Centre of the World'. From here, a network of ancient trails stretched across the Andes and South America, from the equatorial jungles to the plains of modern-day Argentina.

Cuzco reached its zenith of power and influence during the brief flowering of the Inca Empire between 1438 and 1532 AD, but far more ancient myths surround the city's origins.

Cuzco's **architecture** represents a unique blending of cultures, with the cyclopean stone blocks of pre-Colonial structures merging with splendid Baroque churches and manors built on foundations of elaborately carved stone.

Soon after the Spanish conquest, many Inca buildings were looted and demolished and their fabric and foundations were used to build new religious buildings, colonial palaces and mansions.

Cuzco's unique **mestizo culture** has been affected by the advent of tourism, with hundreds of thousands of visitors passing through each year – some of them

DON'T MISS

*** Inca Trail: Peru's most popular adventure trek.
*** Machu Picchu: heart of the ancient Inca empire.
*** Cuzco Cathedral: grand relic of the colonial era.
** La Compañía de Jesús: imposing pile of Spanish heritage.
** Plaza de Armas: the lively centre of life in Cuzco.
** Iglesia Santo Domingo: one of Peru's finest old churches.

Opposite: *Machu Picchu's stone sundial, an indicator of the high level of sophistication of the lost empire of the Incas.*

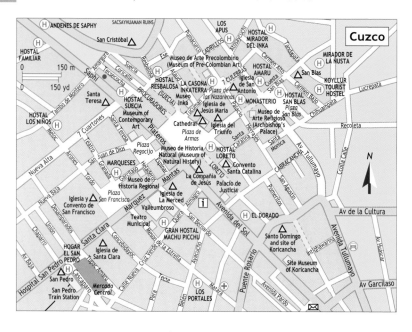

wealthy tourists travelling in five-star luxury, others budget backpackers looking for adrenaline sports such as whitewater rafting as well as a sight of the Inca relics. As a result, the city is arguably the most cosmopolitan spot in Peru.

The **traditional cuisine** of the area is based on combinations of plants native to the region and now familiar worldwide – such as sweetcorn (maize), potatoes and chilli peppers – along with meat such as pork and mutton, brought to Peru by the Spaniards. Cuzco is one of the best places to sample traditional Peruvian cooking, but it also has plenty of international restaurants, five-star hotels, budget hostels, a huge array of street markets and souvenir stores, and dozens of competing tour and sightseeing companies. The city's main thoroughfare, Procuradores, has so many backpackers' hostels, budget restaurants, tour agencies, second-hand bookshps and Internet cafés that it has earned the nickname 'Gringo Alley'.

Cuzco owes its tourism fame to its commanding position at the head of the legendary Inca Trail, which leads visitors to one of the wonders of the world, the lost Inca city of **Machu Picchu**. Shrouded in myth until its rediscovery less than a century ago, this mountain fastness of the Inca is for many the high point of a visit to Peru.

Cuzco
Plaza de Armas
This sweeping plaza is Cuzco's main square and in Inca times was known as Huacaypata (square of the warriors). Today it is surrounded by graceful stone arcades, built in the early colonial era, and by dignified colonial buildings, including the **Cathedral** (on the northeast side of the square) and the church of **La Compañía de Jesús** (on the southeast side). Before the coming of the Spanish, the Plaza was the venue for the most important religious event of the Inca year, **Inti Raymi** (the Festival of the Sun), which is still celebrated today – albeit more as a tourist spectacle than a religious festival.

Remnants of the ancient Inca walls, incorporated into later Spanish colonial buildings, can be seen on either side of **Loreto**, which runs off the southeast corner of the square, and on **Hatan Rumiyoc**, where a 12-cornered block built into the wall of the **Archbishop's Palace** was once part of an Inca palace.

The **San Blas** quarter, with its long, steep paved streets and quiet squares, is Cuzco's artisans' quarter, and many of the region's most highly regarded craftsmen have their homes and workshops in the streets surrounding the 16th-century church of San Blas, among them Hilario Mendivil, Edilberto Merida, Santiago Rojas and Maximiliana Palomino.

Below: *The Plaza de Armas, in the centre of Cuzco, is surrounded by colonial churches and cathedrals, restaurants, bars and souvenir stores.*

Below: *The Cathedral overlooking Cuzco's Plaza de Armas has been damaged by earthquakes, restored, and repaired over several centuries and is one of the city's most prominent landmarks.*

Cathedral ★★★

The Spaniards demolished the Inca fortress of Sacsayhuaman and used their newly converted subjects as slave labour to haul its giant red granite blocks over to the site of their **Cathedral**, constructed between 1560 and 1664. Despite its dubious past, it is perhaps the most immediately impressive building in Cuzco, with a graceful Renaissance façade that sets off the ornate gilt and silverwork of its Baroque interior, which contains lavish gold and silver colonial-era relics, carved wooden altars and some amazing original paintings from the dawn of the Cuzco style of religious art (known as the Escuela Cuzqena or **Cuzco School**), including a fascinating portrayal of the *Last Supper*, *La Ultima Cena*, by Marcos Zapata.

The cathedral is flanked by two smaller chapels. To the right, as you face the building, the **Iglesia del Triunfo** (Church of the Triumph) was the city's first Cathedral. Built in 1539, it stands on the foundations of the **palace of the Inca Viracocha**. To the left is the less impressive **Iglesia de Jesús María**, a relatively recent embellishment which dates from 1733.

The cathedral is open 10:00–11:30 and 14:00–17:30 Monday–Wednesday and Friday–Saturday.

La Compañía de Jesús ★★

Like so many Christian places of worship in Peru, this church, built for the Jesuit order in 1571, is built on the foundations of an older Inca building, in this case the **Amarucancha** or **palace of the Inca Huayna Capac**. With a spectacular, elaborately carved stone façade, it is considered to be one of the finest pieces of Baroque religious architecture in all of South

America, and is especially striking when it is illuminated after dark. Inside, the main altar, with its carved cedarwood and gold leaf, lives up to the impact of the exterior. The church houses a veritable treasury of work by artists of the Cuzco School, including oil paintings on wood and canvas and remarkable stone carvings. The building was virtually demolished by an earthquake in 1650 and was almost completely rebuilt. To one side, the ancient oratory of **San Ignacio de Loyola**, founder of the Jesuit order, is one of the few surviving features of the original building. Open 10:00–11:30 and 14:00–17:30 Monday–Wednesday and Friday–Saturday.

Above: *La Compañia de Jesús, on Cuzco's Plaza de Armas, is one of the most impressive colonial places of worship in Peru.*

Iglesia de la Merced **

This beautiful 16th-century convent and its church have suffered more than most from the earthquakes that have repeatedly rocked Cuzco over the centuries, but its graceful Baroque-Renaissance cloister is one of the loveliest pieces of religious architecture in Peru.

Within are beautifully decorated choir stalls, an array of colonial portraits, and a breathtaking golden tabernacle, 1.3m (3.5ft) in length and studded with gemstones surrounding an enormous pearl in the shape of a mermaid – the second largest pearl ever found. Off Plaza de Armas, it is open 09:00–12:00 and 14:00–17:00 Monday–Saturday.

Museo de Arte Religioso (Archbishop's Palace) **

This remarkable building has had several owners. Built on the foundations of the **palace of the Inca Roca**, it was originally the home of the Marquis de Buenavista, then of the Archbishop of Cuzco. It now houses an enormous collecton of religious art and is very informative on the dealings between the Spanish colonialists and their Indian subjects after the conquest. The grand hall of the archbishop is another highlight. At Hatun Rumiyoc, it is open 08:00–11:30 and 15:00–17:30 Monday–Saturday.

SCULPTED SKULLS

Several of the early pre-Columbian civilizations, including the Huari of Pikillacta and the people of the Paracas culture, practised skull deformation, using cushions, metal straps and boards to apply continuous pressure to malleable infant skulls, broadening and flattening them laterally or creating a cone-like shape. Apparently, this did not affect mental ability. Why they did this is not known, though some wilder explanations include claims that they wanted to imitate the features of visitors from space.

Above: *An exhibit in the Museum of Pre-Colombian Art.*

Convent of Santo Domingo and the Koricancha **

Standing on the site of the Koricancha, the Inca empire's most important sun temple, the Convent of Santo Domingo is a mixture of styles, with a Baroque spire rising from a Renaissance façade. It also has a fine collection of paintings by artists of the Cuzco School. Toppled by earthquakes in 1650 and 1950, and damaged again in 1986, it has each time been rebuilt.

Forming the foundations of the Dominican convent, the remnants of the Inca temple are still impressive, with huge, precisely fitted stone blocks forming the walls, which were once covered with great panels of solid gold – all of which were stripped and melted down by the Spaniards. A small **archaeological museum** (open 09:30–17:30, access from Av. Sol) exhibits Inca relics. Plazoleta Santo Domingo, open 08:30–17:30 Monday–Saturday and 14:00–17:00 Sunday.

Convent of Santa Catalina *

Colonial and religious art, including many works by painters of the Cuzco School, is displayed in this former convent. At Av. Arequipa, it is open 09:00–17:30 Saturday–Thursday, 08:00–16:00 Friday.

Monastery of San Francisco *

This monastery and its church date from the 16th and 17th centuries and compared with the gorgeous Baroque exteriors of most of Cuzco's grand religious buildings this Franciscan foundation looks positively plain, in keeping with the order's austere tradition. A huge but surprisingly uninspiring collection of religious paintings from the colonial era jostles for space on the walls, and the highlight is an enormous family tree of **St Francis of Assisi**, the founder of the order. A slightly gruesome crypt, with skulls and bones arranged as a grim memento mori, may appeal to the more morbid visitor. Plaza San Francisco, open 09:00–16:00 Monday–Friday.

CUZCO MUSEUMS

As well as the collections housed in its great religious buildings, Cuzco also has a number of museums which give insights into many aspects of the region, its history and its natural and man-made heritage.

Museo Inka (Inca Museum) **

This museum is housed in a grand colonial mansion, the former residence of Spanish grandees, and was completely rebuilt after the earthquake of 1950. Within are lavishly decorated walls and ceilings, statues of mythological beasts, and a glittering collection of Inca relics in gold, copper and silver, ceramics, weavings, Inca mummies and painted wooden goblets. Located on the corner of Tucuman and Ataud, it is open 09:00–17:00 Monday–Friday, 09:00–16:00 Saturday.

Museum of Pre-Colombian Art *

This museum opened in 2003 and displays a collection of almost 500 pieces of jewellery, pottery, stone-carving and weaving from pre-Conquest Peru, most of which come from the huge collection of Lima's **Museo Rafael Larco Herrera** (*see* page 41). Located on Plaza de las Nazarenas, it is open daily 09:00–22:00.

Below: *Cuzco women in traditional costume weave colourful fabrics in the courtyard of Cuzco's Inca Museum.*

Museum of Regional History *

Displays laid out in chronological order highlight each era of Peruvian and Andean history, from the earliest hunter-gatherer cultures through the rise of the Chavín civilization to the present day. At Plaza Regocijo (corner of Calle Garcilaso and Heladeros), it is open 08:00–17:00 Monday–Saturday.

Museum of Natural History *

This eclectic museum is a taxidermists's dream, with stuffed animals and birds of the Andes along with dioramas and displays which attempt to give some insight into the the natural habitats and environment of Cuzco and the surrounding region. Plaza de Armas, open 09:30–12:00 and 15:00–18:00 Monday–Friday.

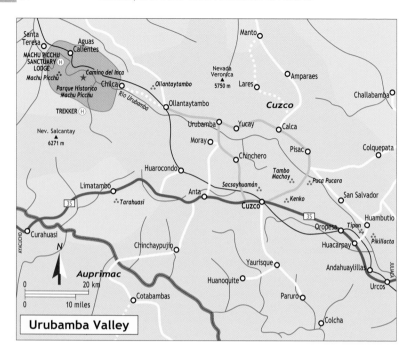

Urubamba Valley

URUBAMBA VALLEY

Cuzco is the gateway to the Urubamba Valley, also known as the **Sacred Valley of the Incas**. Overlooked by the summits of the Vilcanota mountain range, it lies only an hour's drive from Cuzco. Terraced mountainsides are evidence of long centuries of painstaking cultivation, and since Inca times the valley and its rural communities have supplied Cuzco with most of its farm produce – including maize cobs which are claimed to have the largest kernels in the world. The valley's picturesque **Quechua villages** are highly photogenic, as are its landscapes, and its climate and terrain attract river rafters, mountain bikers and hang-gliding enthusiasts as well as walkers. The **Urubamba River** flows in a northwesterly direction for

Below: *The valley of the Urubamba River shapes the heartland of the Sacred Valley of the Incas.*

some 60km (37 miles) between Rumicolca in the southeast towards Ollantaytambo, Chilca and the start of the Inca Trail, flowing some 20km (16 miles) north of the city of Cuzco.

NORTHWEST FROM CUZCO
Sacsayhuaman ***
About 6km (4 miles) north of central Cuzco, three large terraces defended by great stone battlements up to 300m (1000ft) in length make up this enormous **Inca military site**, which was built to guard Cuzco and its treasures against invasion from the east. This is one of the most impressive of the Inca fortresses, with zig-zag ramparts overlooked by massive towers, and was manned in time of war by a 5000-strong garrison. Many of its stones were looted by the Spanish, who used them to build several of their colonial buildings in nearby Cuzco

Above: *The massive stone battlements of Sacsayhuaman, north of Cuzco, were built to defend the Inca capital against invasion.*

Kenko *
This **temple site** on the outskirts of Cuzco (2km/1 mile east of Sacsayhuaman) stands on a limestone crag which the Inca carved out into tunnels, galleries and a hillside amphitheatre.

Puca Pucara *
Less than 1km (0.6 miles) east of Kenko are the red stone ramparts of Puca Pucara, a bastion of Cuzco's huge and complex system of defences. Its stone stairs, terraces and red sandstone walls offer superb views of the surrounding valley.

Tambo Machay **
Channels and aqueducts carved from the living rock lend credence to the belief that this Inca site was a royal hideaway surrounded by lush, artificially irrigated gardens as well as a temple dedicated to the worship of

INTI RAYMI

Inti Raymi, the midsummer festival that dates back to the time of the Incas, is Peru's greatest annual event. An actor representing the Inca ruler is carried in procession, from the site of Cuzco's Koricancha sun temple to the terraces below Sacsayhuaman, 2km (1 mile) from central Cuzco, where thousands of actors in Inca costume re-enact the ceremony of sun-worship, then ascend to Sacsayhuaman for the ritual sacrifice of two llamas. Several days of feasting, music and dance follow the main event.

water as a sacred element. With its ceremonial baths and cascades of mountain water, it is also known as the **Baños del Inca** or Inca baths.

Pisac **

This small town of 2000 people is 32km (20 miles) from Cuzco. Its attractions include one of the region's most important Inca sites, an old quarter dating from the pre-Colonial era and a 'modern' quarter of colonial buildings that still exude a certain faded grandeur. Visit on a Sunday, when the weekly market attracts thousands of people from remote mountain villages in colourful traditional costume (as well as hundreds of less traditionally dressed sightseers). The Inca citadel is 5km (3 miles) north of the village, a steep two-hour hike on foot (or a 10km/6-mile taxi ride on a paved road). Built to command access to the Urubamba Valley, the large site of the fortress city is surrounded by terraced fields and its stone temples are well preserved. Open 07:00–16:00 daily.

Chinchero *

A colourful Sunday market where traders sell authentic handicrafts and weavings in the style of the Inca period is the main attraction of this small community 3762m (12,343ft) above sea level and 28km (17 miles) northwest of Cuzco, en route to Urubamba and the Inca Trail. Chinchero also has some Inca ruins, including the remains of terraces which surrounded the **palace of Tupac Inca Yupanqui**, as well as a colonial church built on Inca foundations.

Moray *

Moray is a tribute to the agricultural science of the Inca, with its four circular terraces which were watered

PUCARA BULLS

The Pucara region, between Cuzco and Juliaca, is famed for its luck-bringing ceramic bulls, known as *toritos* ('little bulls'). Most are made in the village of Santiago de Pupaya, and the *torito* is linked to the centuries-old festival of Senalacuy, when cattle are herded together for branding and the most handsome bull is selected to sire next year's calves. Ochre spiral patterns are painted on the chosen bull's hide, chilli peppers are rubbed under his tail and nose, and the unfortunate bull is then urged to canter around the village while being pelted with flowers and fruit.

using a complex system of canals and gutters and where the Inca grew more than 250 kinds of crop, including corn, potatoes, quinoa and kiwicha.

Urubamba *

Urubamba is, as its name implies, the valley's capital, with more than 8000 inhabitants. Overlooked by the 5750m (18,000ft) summit of **Nevado Veronica**, it is surrounded by magnificent scenery and has plenty of places to stay and eat, making it a good stop-off on the way to the Inca Trail or a base for leisurely exploration of the Valley, but is otherwise unexciting.

Ollantaytambo **

Ollantaytambo, situated 21km (14 miles) northwest of Urubamba, is the last sizeable community before the beginning of the Inca Trail and is studded with hotels, restaurants and trekking and tour agencies. But the village is more than just functional: it has an array of archaeological sights worth seeing, including the stone walls of **Hanan Haucaypata**, just to the north of the central plaza.

On the slopes above the village, among the vast terraces sculpted from the hillside, stand the imposing **Temple of the Sun**, the **Royal Hall** and remnants of a number of other **Inca structures**. The Inca complex is open to the public from 07:00–18:00 daily.

MIXED BLESSING

The eucalyptus tree – an import from Australia – is planted on wasteland and hillsides across Peru. Tolerant of low rainfall and poor soil, it grows quickly, helps to prevent erosion, and provides a ready source of wood for fuel and building. But eucalyptus is a very mixed blessing – it quickly strips all nutrients from the soil, making it useless for other cultivation.

Opposite: *Pisac, one of the most important Inca sites, is renowned for its vibrant Sunday market.* **Below:** *Ollantaytambo, close to the beginning of the Inca Trail, is surrounded by centuries-old agricultural terraces.*

SOUTHEAST FROM CUZCO

Tipon ★★

Tipon, 20km (12 miles) southeast of Cuzco, is believed to have been an **Inca palace** surrounded by royal gardens. As at Tambo Machay, the Inca probably worshipped water here, and the site, with its cunningly arrayed aqueducts, waterfalls and channels, indicates how well the Inca had mastered the science of hydraulics. Open 24/7.

Pikillacta ★★

Pikillacta, 32km (20 miles) southeast of Cuzco, was built more than 1000 years ago by the pre-Inca Huari (or Wari) culture and the stonework of this fortress-city is notably less skilled than the fortresses and temples of the Inca. Opposite the main site and 1km (0.6 miles) east is a huge Inca ceremonial gateway, the **Rumicolca**, built on the foundations of a Huari building and displaying the much greater skills of the Inca masons.

THE INCA TRAIL ★★★

The legendary Inca Trail is the best preserved and most famous section of the vast and complex network of 23,000km (14,000 miles) of stone-paved mountain roads that the Inca built to tie together the remotest regions of their vast Andean empire. Without either wheeled transport or draught animals, goods were carried by pack-llamas or human porters. Sophisticated systems of ramps and stairs carried the **Qhapaq Nan** (King's Highway) up steep mountainsides, and canyons and river gorges were crossed on hanging bridges.

Hiking the 43km (26-mile) Inca Trail takes you back in time and carries the walker through awe-inspiring scenery and a variety of ecosystems and microclimates. Wildlife

to be seen on the way includes flocks of wild llama, vicuña and vizcacha, the brilliantly coloured Andean cock-of-the-rocks, rare spectacled bears and hundreds of flower and tree species. It also passes Inca temples and fortresses including **Wiñay Wayna** and **Phuyupatamarca**, built centuries ago as outposts along the royal highway. At its lowest level, the trail drops to 2600m (8530ft) above sea level, and climbs at its highest point over the Warmimanuska pass at an altitude of about 4200m (13,776ft). The Inca Trail starts at **Qorihuayrachina**, at Km 88 of the Cuzco-Quillabamba Railway, and takes three to four days, requiring a high level of fitness.

About 25 miles (40 km) southeast of Cuzco, the serene 17th-century Baroque church at **Andahuaylillas**, with its fine mural paintings and statues, is a welcome contrast to the overblown interiors of so many of Peru's colonial churches.

The trail ends at **Intipunku**, the 'Gateway of the Sun', which opens directly onto the ruins of Machu Picchu.

MACHU PICCHU ★★★

Machu Picchu is the most evocative of all the great Inca sites and ranks among the marvels of the ancient world, not only because of the skills of its builders but also because of its breathtaking surroundings.

Built during the reign of the Inca Tupac Yupanqui at a time when the Inca Empire was at its zenith, Machu Picchu is surrounded by a 32,492km^2 (12,542 sq mile) natural reserve which was declared a UNESCO World Cultural and Natural Heritage Site in 1983.

The site is situated 120km (74 miles) from Cuzco, perched amongst cloud-capped crags that soar above the valley of the Urubamba River at an altitude of 2400m (7872ft) above sea level, and is divided into two sections: the urban area, including the ruins of temples,

Above: *The Inca trail is part of a vast network of ancient mountain roads.*
Opposite: *Cunningly designed channels and waterfalls at Tipon are evidence of the architectural skills of the Inca builders.*

BOULDER ART

On the highest hills above almost every Peruvian town, you may see slogans, numbers and letters picked out in white boulders. These are the work of schools, colleges and army regiments, who take pride in creating the most prominent landmark for their outfit.

Above: *Aerial view of Machu Picchu ruins.*

Holiday Reading

There are very few English-language bookshops in Peru, but new and second-hand books, including fiction by leading Peruvian and Latin American authors in translation, paperback novels, guidebooks and non-fiction works can be found in Lima, Cuzco and Arequipa.
Norton's Bar, next to the Compañía church on Cuzco's Plaza de Armas, has its own used paperback exchange (two for one). In Arequipa, **Librería el Lector** (San Francisco 221) has an excellent choice of new and used books. In Lima's Miraflores district, **Ibero Librerías** on the Ovalo (next to the Incahaus hostel) sells new fiction and non-fiction books.

palaces, stone stairways and fountains, and the surrounding agricultural terraces which supplied the ancient city and which are in themselves a remarkable testament to the skill, ingenuity and energy of their Inca builders.

Machu Picchu is often referred to as a 'lost city' but of course it was nothing of the kind. While the Spanish colonials had lost all knowledge of its whereabouts, the Quechua people of this remote valley had known of its existence for centuries, and it was a local guide, **Melchior Arteaga**, who led the American archaeologist **Hiram Bingham** to the site in 1911. Bingham, a professor at Yale University, returned three years later with a team of archaeologists funded by Yale and the rediscovery of Machu Picchu began.

Bingham's research revealed that the citadel had been mainly a place of worship, and the discovery of a cemetery that appeared to have been used only for the interment of women led him to conjecture that Machu Picchu was a vast convent of *ajillas* (temple virgins). Later research, using more sophisticated methods, revealed that the skeletons found in the cemetery were both male and female, refuting Bingham's hypothesis. The citadel is now thought to have been a rural retreat for the Inca rulers, and to have been abandoned after the fall of Cuzco and the empire to the Spaniards.

The ruins are extremely popular, and start to become crowded in the mornings from around 10:00. Within the perimeter of the site, key features include the **House of the Guardian of the Funerary Rock**, one of the few buildings to have been fully restored. Other high points include the **Sacred Baths**, the **Temple of the Sun** with its round tower, the **Sacred Square** (from which there are magnificent views of the surrounding Andean peaks), the **Temple of the Three Windows**, the **Principal Temple** and the **House of the High Priest**. A stairway leads to the main temple site, the **Intihuatana**, with a sculpted pillar used by Inca sun-priests to predict the dates of the annual solstices. The central square separates the sacred pre-cincts from the more workaday part of Machu Picchu – the storehouses, workshops and workers' homes.

For an even more breathtaking view, follow the path from the central square of Machu Picchu to the top of the adjacent crag, **Huayna Picchu** (open 07:00–14:00). This steep walk takes about one hour to 90 minutes. The ruins are open from 06:00–21:30 daily.

Aguas Calientes (Machu Picchu Pueblo)

This small village in the forest approximately 8km (5miles) from Machu Picchu is a popular place for trav-ellers to stay overnight while visiting the ruins. The village has a number of budget guesthouses as well as some more luxurious hotels.

The spectacular four-hour tourist train route from Cuzco arrives at the new, purpose-built Aguas Calientes station, while local trains leave from the older station in the centre of town. For times and details, visit the website www.perurail.com

Around 15 minutes' walk from the town centre are several thermal springs (open daily 05:00–21:00, admission US$3, bring your own towel) and the summit of Putucusi (a demanding trek taking two hours each way) on the opposite side of the Vilcanota River has amaz-ing views across the valley to Machu Picchu.

> **BANNED ABROAD**
>
> Despite its undoubted therapeutic properties and popularity in Peru as a mild stimulant and cure for moun-tain sickness, *mate de coca* (coca leaf tea) is listed as an illegal substance in most of Europe and North America. Those planning to drive soon after arriving home should avoid drinking *mate de coca* for a couple of days before leaving Peru – if you are unlucky enough to be drug-tested after an accident, you may test positive for cocaine, coca's much more powerful and illegal derivative.

Below: *For less energetic travellers, the tourist train ride from Cuzco to Aguas Calientes is the easiest way to get to Machu Picchu.*

Cuzco, the Inca Trail and Machu Picchu at a Glance

BEST TIMES TO VISIT

Avoid the region during the cold, rainy months (Nov–Mar), when temperatures average 12°C (54°F). The dry season, May–Oct, is the recommended time to visit, with sunny, dry days, chilly nights and an average temperature of 9°C (48°F). Pack warm clothing, sunscreen and a hat.

GETTING THERE

Cuzco is just over 1000km (640 miles) from Lima and 450km (280 miles) from Arequipa. There are several **flights** daily from Lima (one hour), Arequipa (30 mins) and Juliaca (30 mins). There are frequent **buses** from Lima and Arequipa. **Trains** leave from the Huanchac Station (Avenida Sol, tel: (084) 23 87 22, reservas@perurail.com) for Urcos, Sicuani, Juliaca and Puno, and from the San Pedro Station (next to the Central Market, tel: (084) 22 19 92) for Ollantaytambo and Machu Picchu. Three tourist trains leave Cuzco for Machu Picchu daily, taking around four hours.

GETTING AROUND

Cuzco's airport is 2km (1.25 miles) from the centre of town. Taxis and *colectivos* operate between airport and town. Cuzco is small enough to be most easily explored on foot, but there are also local buses, taxis and a tourist tram, the Tranvia, tel: (084) 22 43 77, which makes a two-

hour round trip of the city, visiting Sacsayhuaman, the San Blas craftsmen's district and other highlights. It leaves twice daily at 10:00 and 13:00 from the Plaza de Armas. To walk the **Inca Trail** you must reserve with one of the specially licensed tour companies at least 30 days in advance as only 500 people (including guides and porters) may walk the trail at any one time. Reservations can be made up to one year ahead. Payment must be made in advance. Further information and a list of licensed trekking agencies can be found at www.inc-cusco.gob.pe or from the Commission for the Promotion of Peru, Calle Uno Oeste 050, San Isidro, Lima, tel: 224 3131, www.peru.org.pe

WHERE TO STAY

LUXURY
Hotel Monasterio, Palacio 136, Cuzco, tel: (084) 24 17 77, www.monasterio.orient-express.com The Monasterio de San Antonio Abad, built in 1592, is a national historic landmark. Beautifully converted into a hotel in 1995, it has 126 rooms – some 'oxygen-enriched' for those suffering altitude sickness – around a stunning cloistered courtyard.
Machu Picchu Sanctuary Lodge, Machu Picchu Ruins, tel: (084) 98 16 956, www. machupicchu.orient-express.com
One of the most luxurious (and

expensive) hotels in Peru, the Sanctuary Lodge is the only hotel next to the ruins. The hotel has 29 rooms and two suites, all with private bathrooms, cable TV and VCR, minibar and safety deposit. The restaurant serves international and Peruvian dishes.
Inkaterra Machu Picchu Hotel, Aguas Calientes, tel: (051) 16 10 0400, www.inkaterra.com
A collection of stone cottages with red-tiled roofs amid lush, subtropical foliage – more than 130 species of bird can be seen in its gardens and it stands close to the banks of the fast flowing Urubamba River. All 86 rooms have stone-tiled floors and en-suite bathrooms and the attractive restaurant and outdoor patio have fabulous views.

MID-RANGE
Andenes de Saphy, Saphy 848, Cuzco tel: (084) 22 75 61, www.andenesdesaphi.com This comfortable hotel in a colonial mansion with three flower-filled terraces is 300m from the Plaza de Armas.
Gringo Bill's Hotel, Colla Raymi 104, Plaza de Armas, Aguas Calientes, tel: 21 10 46, www.gringobills.com The best base for exploring Machu Picchu (8km/ 5 miles away) or resting up after the Inca Trail hike, with clean and comfortable rooms, en-suite hot showers, a good restaurant and helpful staff.

Cuzco, the Inca Trail and Machu Picchu at a Glance

BUDGET

Hostal Imperial Palace, Calle Tecsecocha 490B, Cuzco, tel: (084) 22 33 24. Clean, comfortable two-star hostel with ten rooms, two blocks from the Plaza de Armas, at the high end of the budget scale.

Hostales los Niños, Meloc 442, Cuzco, tel: (084) 23 14 24, www.ninoshotel.com These two prize-winning hotels are run as a charity and the profits are used to give hot meals, showers, medical and dental assistance and educational help to local children in need. Accommodation is in stylish, fully renovated old buildings and each hotel has a large sunny patio. Highly recommended.

Ninos Apartments, contact details same as Hostales los Ninos. Four apartments on the same street as the second Ninos hotel and within walking distance of the Plaza de Armas. Shared shower and WC, fully equipped kitchen, and use of Ninos hotel facilities including laundry, café and luggage store. Daily and monthly rates, perfect for those planning a longer stay in the Cuzco area.

Hostal Casa de Campo, Tandapata 296, Cuzco, tel: (084) 24 44 04, www.hotel casadecampo.com In the picturesque San Blas district, the large rooms have great views, a garden and a big lounge with a fireplace. The hotel offers free airport pick-up if required.

LUXURY

Restaurant El Paititi, Portal Carrizos 270, Cuzco, tel: (084) 25 26 86. Probably Cuzco's most elegant restaurant; Inca walls and live traditional or classical music in the evening.

Inka Grill, Portal de Panes 115, Cuzco, tel: (084) 26 29 92. The speciality in this Peruvian restaurant is roast guinea pig; order it one day in advance. Inka Grill also has Peruvian favourites and less challenging international dishes.

Machu Picchu El Pueblo Hotel (see Where to Stay), Aguas Calientes. The most elegant spot to eat in Aguas Calientes, with very generous lunch and dinner buffets.

MID-RANGE

Greens, Tandapata 700, Cuzco, tel: (084) 24 38 20. San Blas is an unlikely place to find a restaurant serving English Sunday roasts, as well as curries, steaks and pasta but Greens does just that. Highly recommended.

Toto's House, Imperio de los Incas, Aguas Calientes, tel: (084) 21 10 20. Good buffet meals with river views.

Indio Feliz, Lloque Yupanque Loti, Aguas Calientes, tel: (084) 21 10 90. Excellent service, cooking with a French accent.

BUDGET

Chez Maggi La Antigua, Procuradores 344, Cuzco, tel: (084) 23 48 61. This Gringo Alley favourite has branches at Procuradores 365 and 374 as well as in Aguas Calientes, but this is the original; pizza, salads, pasta and live music.

Airport: iPeru, airport arrivals halls, tel: (084) 23 7364, email: iperucusco@promperu.gob.pe **Cuzco:** iPeru, 102 Galerias Turisticas, Av. Sol 103, tel: (084) 25 2974. **Machu Picchu:** iPeru, Edificio del Instituto Nacional de Cultura, tel: (084) 21 1140.

South American Explorers Club, Choquechaca 188, tel: (084) 24 54 84, e-mail: cuscoclub@saexplorers.org **Andean Travel Web**, Calle Garcilaso 265, 2nd floor, Cuzco, www.andeantravel web.com/peru Brilliant website, everything you need to plan your Peru trip.

CUZCO	J	F	M	A	M	J	J	A	S	O	N	D
AVERAGE TEMP. °F	68	69	70	71	70	69	70	70	71	72	73	71
AVERAGE TEMP. °C	20	21	21	22	21	21	21	21	22	22	23	22
RAINFALL in	6.4	5.9	4.3	2	0.6	0.2	0.2	0.4	1	2.6	3	5.4
RAINFALL mm	163	150	109	51	15	5	5	10	25	66	76	137
DAYS OF RAINFALL	18	13	11	8	3	2	2	2	7	8	12	16

4
Lake Titicaca

South of **Cuzco**, the Andes sweep towards Peru's border with Bolivia and the inland sea of Lake Titicaca, the highest navigable body of water in the world. To the north, the **Cordillera Vilcanota**, **Cordillera Carabaya** and **Cordillera Apolobamba** ranges descend to the valleys and tropical forests that surround the tributaries of the **Río Madre de Dios**, which flows east across the border into Bolivia. Across the border, the **Cordillera Real** dominates the eastern shore of Titicaca. To the west of the lake, steep valleys descend to the arid coastal plains.

Many visitors see little more of the region than **Puno** and the famed **floating islands** before travelling on to Cuzco or southward across Lake Titicaca, but the lake repays a longer stay in order to spend time absorbing the colourful **Aymara culture** of the lakeside villages and the unique way of life of the lake islanders, which is still largely unpolluted by tourism.

Although Puno and Lake Titicaca feature on many tourist itineraries and are a popular stop for travellers who are heading onward to Bolivia, the Titicaca region is generally far less commercialized than Cuzco and the Inca Trail, and many authentic folk customs and festivals are preserved in and around Juliaca, Puno and other towns and villages. Travelling by road between Cuzco and Puno, it is worth stopping at the Inca site of **Raqchi**, where huge stone columns once held up the huge roof of the Temple of Viracocha. There are spectacular views from the pass at **La Roya**, more than 4000m (13,124ft)

DON'T MISS

*** Lake Titicaca:** jade green inland sea surrounded by bare mountain slopes.
*** Floating Islands:** reed rafts that support a unique, centuries-old community.
** Taquile:** the perfect anti-dote to the tourist trail.

Opposite: *Motor launches connect Lake Titicaca's island settlements with the mainland port of Puno.*

TITICACA STATISTICS

Length: 170km (110 miles)
Width: 60km (38 miles)
Surface area: 8300km² (3205 sq miles) of which 4700km² (1815 sq miles) is in Peru
Depth: 275m (902ft) at its deepest
Altitude: 3820m (12,500ft) above sea level

above sea level, which marks the transition from the cordillera valleys to the Altiplano country.

JULIACA *

Juliaca, the largest town in Puno province, is of little interest except as a transport junction for travellers en route between Arequipa, Cuzco and Puno. It has the province's only airport, and road transport from Arequipa connects here with buses and trains between Puno and Cuzco. If you have to stay overnight, it has an adequate supply of comfortable hotels, guesthouses and places to eat – and because few tourists do stay for long, local market traders are more open to offers than most. It's a good place to shop for locally made alpaca

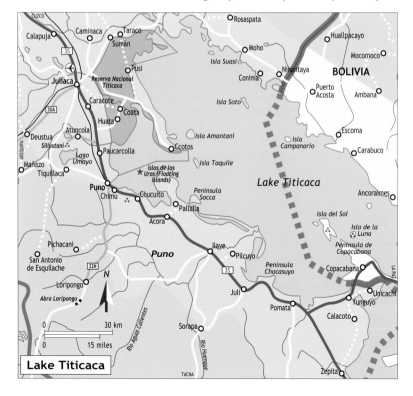

Lake Titicaca

wool hats, clothes and wall-hangings. Try the Monday market on the **Plaza Melgar**, or the daily handicrafts market at **Plaza Bolognesi**, for bargains. **Sillustani**, 15 minutes off the main road midway between Juliaca and Puno, is famous for its *chullpas* (burial towers) which are among the few visible relics of the pre-Inca **Waru culture** which flourished around Lake Titicaca.

Puno *

On the Peruvian side, the lakeside port of Puno – 3827m (12,552ft) above sea level – is the main base for exploring this unique inland sea and travelling onward, with antiquated ferries plying across the lake to the Bolivian shore. Puno is admittedly a bit of a visual let-down when compared to its grand surroundings. Its buildings are mostly drab and functional – though it has a sprinkling of colonial relics such as the Baroque **Cathedral** on the Plaza de Armas, dating from 1757, and the **Casa del Corregidor**, a picturesque 17th-century mansion that now serves as Puno's Cultural Centre. If you have time to kill, the shabby little **Maritime Museum**, at the corner of Carrer el Sol and Carrer el Puerto, outlines the history of shipping on the lake from the reed boats (*see* panel, page 99) made famous by Thor Heyerdahl's Ra expedition to the Clyde-built steamships that were hauled up from the coast in sections to be re-assembled in Puno to ply the lake. One of these historic vessels, the *Yavari*, launched in 1870, has been rescued and restored as a floating museum which is normally moored opposite the Sonesta Posada Hotel, about 5km (3 miles) from central Puno, but which sometimes makes voyages across Titicaca under its own steam.

Above: *Colonial buildings in Puno's main square.*

EATING OUT IN PUNO

Some of Puno's best restaurants are to be found along Calle Lima, the main thoroughfare. The town has a good choice of budget eating places – it's hard to spend more than $10 for a meal anywhere – but no outstanding luxury eating places. Be prepared for the apperance each evening of local groups of musicians who wander from restaurant to restaurant, passing the hat round at the end of their performance.

Above: *This tourist boat is made from reeds using traditional skills, but its design is novel.*

LAKE TITICACA ★★★

The jade-green waters of Lake Titicaca, lying 3810m (12,500ft) above sea level, are fringed by thick reed beds and dotted with floating island-villages. The lake, approximately 170km (110 miles) long by 60km (38 miles) wide, is the largest in the Americas and one of the largest on the planet, and the border between Peru and Bolivia bisects its waters from Ninantaya on the northern shore to Copacabana on the southern shore. Surrounding the lake are the treeless, ochre and umber slopes of the Altiplano region where Peru meets upland Bolivia.

For the two largest ethnic groups of pre-Colonial Peru, the **Quechua** and **Aymara** peoples, Titicaca was a sacred place, and according to Inca tradition the founders of the Inca civilization, **Manco Capac** and **Mama Ocllo**, emerged from the waters of Titicaca to create their culture. While Quechua and Aymara people still make up a substantial part of Peru's population, the same cannot be said of Titicaca's other indigenous group, the **Uros**, who cling to an ancient way of life on their floating islands of reeds and in villages along the northern shores of the lake. Similarly fragile and unique are the cultures of Titicaca's fixed islands – **Taquile**, **Amantani** and **Suasi** – with their ancient agricultural systems and social order.

Titicaca is a **national nature reserve** which harbours more than a dozen species of freshwater fish, numerous bird and mammal species and – unique to the lake – the Titicaca giant frog (*see* panel, page 70). Northeast of the lake (beyond the Bolivian border), the **Cordillera Real** makes a stunning backdrop.

Floating Islands (Islas Flotantes or Uros Islands) ***

Puno sits at the head of an almost landlocked bay, within two jutting peninsulas. In the shallow waters of this lagoon, a unique way of life has evolved. The Uros people who inhabit Lake Titicaca's floating islands abandoned dry land more than six centuries ago to escape the continual warfare between the expanding Inca and the lakeside Colla tribes. Like the Venetians of medieval Europe, they created a unique island culture – except that the islands of the Uros are not fixed, but are vast floating rafts made from the *totora* reeds which grow in the broad shallows of the lake margins. They are maintained by piling fresh reeds on the upper layers of each island as the lower layers disintegrate. There are more than 40 of these floating communities, where the Uros people live in reed huts, fish for *carrache* (a small lake fish) travel between islands and the mainland in boats woven from reeds, and make much of their cash income by selling woven reed artefacts to visitors. Paintings on ceramics, and other archaeological evidence, indicate that their homes and boats have not changed for more than 1000 years. The Uros number only a few hundred. Those living on the islands closest to Puno are accustomed to frequent tourist visits, while more authetic (but less welcoming) island lifestyles can be found on the islands furthest from Puno, isolated by a maze of shallow channels and visitable only with a privately chartered boat. Boats to the main island leave Puno irregularly from around 07:00 (they leave when full) until around 12:00; tickets are sold on board or at the quayside. Excursion boats, bookable through Puno travel agencies, leave several times daily for a guided two-hour

Below: *Floating villages near Puno are tourist attractions, but others do not welcome visitors.*

GIANT FROGS

The Titicaca giant frog can grow to 60cm (2ft) in length and weigh up to 1kg (2.2lb). Outstandingly adapted to its unique environment (its wrinkled skin helps it absorb oxygen from water to stay submerged for long periods and also protects it from ultraviolet radiation), the Titicaca frog lives only in the waters of the lake. The Convention on International Trade in Endangered Species (CITES) lists it as vulnerable, but frogs' legs can be found on tourist menus, and 'frog juice' – made by throwing a live frog into a blender with water and honey – has a reputation as an aphrodisiac, known as 'Peruvian Viagra'.

Below: *Terraced fields and eucalyptus trees on Isla Taquile create a landscape that looks almost Mediterranean.*

cruise through the islands, and boats can be chartered privately for longer trips at around $20 per day.

Isla Taquile ★★

Titicaca also has a number of natural islands, of which the easiest to reach is Taquile, a four-hour boat journey from Puno. Around 6km (4 miles) long, Taquile is inhabited by around 2000 **Quechua** islanders who make their living from fishing and herding. It is possible to stay overnight in local homes, and there are several small restaurants in the main village which offer simple meals (mainly fish from the lake and fresh vegetables), but Taquile is definitely for those who prefer the simple life: there is a very limited electrical supply (lighting only), no hot water, no potable water supply and no indoor plumbing – but for a hardy few, the journey, the views across the lake, and a glimpse of an almost untainted traditional way of life make these minor hardships worthwhile.

Isla Amantani ★★

Larger, further from Puno and more populous (with around 4000 inhabitants), Isla Amantani also offers the opportunity to stay in simple village homes with local people. Several Puno travel agencies arrange day trips and overnight stays.

Isla Suasi ★

A stone's throw from the north shore of the lake and easily reached from the north coast village of Conima, tiny Isla Suasi is a good deal more upscale than its neighbours, with a recently built boutique hotel (*see* Where to Stay, page 71) offering lake trips and tours to out-of-the-way villages.

Lake Titicaca at a Glance

Rainy season is from Jan–Mar. The best time to go is from Apr–Sep, with strong sunshine (wear sunscreen), chilly breezes and cold nights.

Daily **flights** from Lima (one hour) and Arequipa (30 minutes) to Juliaca Airport (one hour by road from Puno). **Trains** between Cuzco and Puno take around 10 hours. **Buses** from Cuzco take six hours; buses from Arequipa take five hours. **Catamaran ferries** cross Lake Titicaca to the Bolivian port of Huatajata, with **coach** connections to La Paz (capital of Bolivia); the total journey time is 12 hours. It is possible to travel to/from La Paz by **bus** and **shared taxi**, taking around five hours.

Buses and **shared taxis** connect Puno and Juliaca with smaller towns and villages. Tour companies in Puno offer escorted tours and lake voyages. Boats to the lake islands, mostly operated by the islanders themselves, leave each morning from the Puno quayside. Buy tickets on board.

LUXURY
Libertador Lake Titicaca Puno, Isla Esteves, tel: (051) 36 77 80, www.libertador.com.pe The most luxurious hotel in

the area (with prices to match) on a private island near Puno. **Sonesta Posada del Inca**, Sequicentenario 610, Puno, tel: (051) 36 41 11, www. sonestaperu.com Medium-sized lakeside hotel about 5km (3 miles) from downtown Puno. Very comfortable and with a pleasant location.

MID-RANGE
Posada Don Giorgio, Tarapaca 238, Puno, tel: (051) 36 36 48, e-mail: dongorgio@titicacalake.com Welcoming small hotel, all mod cons, in centre of Puno. **Hotel Ferrocarril**, Av. de la Torre 185, Puno, tel: (051) 36 17 52, www.hotelferrocarril. com Built in 1899 but blandly modernized recently, this hotel is handily located next to the station for those arriving by train. **Isla Suasi**, Conima, tel: (051) 36 59 68, www.islasuasi.com This unique hotel on a private island is built from local materials; sauna, gardens, and boat trips on the lake. **Hotel Titilaka**, tel (051) 1610 0400, www.inkaterra.com New 18-room lodge on a private peninsula beside the lake with fantastic views. Great base for exploring Lake Titicaca.

BUDGET
Totorani Inn, Av. de la Torre 463, tel: (051) 36 45 35, www.totrani.com Well-run, clean, comfortable small hotel, handily located.

Isla Taquile
Locals offer simple accommodation in their homes (cold water and outside toilets) at budget prices and meet visitors at the top of the stairway from the pier to the village centre. Bring a sleeping bag.

Isla Amantani
Islanders here also offer simple accommodation and meet boats from Puno on arrival.

BUDGET
Restaurant Don Piero, Lima 364, tel: (051) 36 59 43. Live traditional music every evening, a favourite with locals, and serves a good array of traditional Peruvian dishes. **Plaza Restaurant**, Puno 425, tel: (051) 35 14 24. Fine fish dishes straight from the lake. **Ukuku's**, Lima 332, tel: (051) 36 73 73. Good local dishes, also pizza, pasta and burgers. The price is very modest.

Isla Taquile and Isla Amantani
Small, simple restaurants serve a limited menu, usually lake fish and local vegetables.

Allways Travel, Tacna 234, Puno, tel: (051) 35 55 52, www.titicacaperu.com **Edgar Adventures**, Jr. Lima 328, Puno, tel: (051) 35 34 44, edgaradventures@terra.com.pe **Piramide Tours**, Jr. Deza 129, tel: (051) 36 73 02, www.titikakalake.com

WINE FESTIVAL

Like those of neighbouring Chile, Peru's homegrown wines have improved enormously in recent years. You can sample them on the spot at the annual International Wine Harvest Festival (which takes place in the first half of March) in and around Ica, with wine and pisco tastings, concerts, dancing and parades.

culture, with a rich heritage of music and craftsmanship, and throughout the south there are relics of the **Inca**, **Nazca** and other vanished civilizations.

ICA

The coastal province of Ica extends to the south of Lima. Much of the southern part of the province is semidesert, and from the Paracas National Reserve south of Pisco to Bahia San Nicolás close to the border of Arequipa province the rugged coast and its arid hinterland are almost uninhabited, and the Pan-America Highway loops far inland.

Despite its seemingly barren landscapes, parts of the province have a near-Mediterranean climate. Ica is known for its **vineyards**, which produce grapes from which both wine and Peru's national drink – the clear grape spirit known as pisco – are made.

Pucusana *

Only 68km (42 miles) south of Lima, this small fishing village-cum-beach-resort is a pleasant enough place to stop on the way south but owes its popularity more to its proximity to Lima than to its beaches, which are adequate but hardly world class.

Below: *Pacific black-backed gulls are among the many sea birds found in the waters off Paracas.*

Cerro Azul *

This exposed beach, about 15km (9 miles) north of the dull coastal town of San Vicente de Cañete, is favoured by Peruvian surfers who travel the 130km (75 miles) south from Lima to ride its breakers.

Pisco *

Pisco, 235km (138 miles) south of Lima, is a small seaport town. With a few small hotels, it is a handy stopping point on the coast highway and is the gateway to the richly biodiverse Paracas National Reserve.

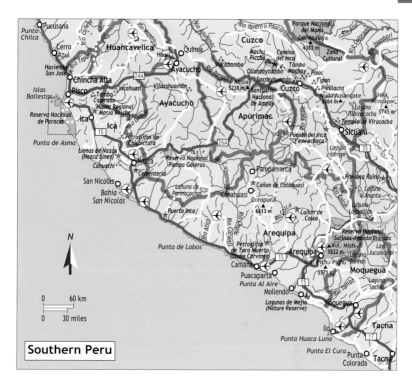

Southern Peru

Paracas National Reserve **

The Paracas National Reserve, 22km (15 miles) south of
Pisco on the Pan-American Highway, covers some
335,000ha (827,450 acres) of desert hinterland, islands,
beaches and sea cliffs that shelter **sea mammals** including dolphins, sperm whales and sealions, and **sea birds**
including pelicans, flamingoes, penguins and cormorants. Around an hour offshore, the **Islas Ballestas**
are protected nesting grounds for vast numbers of
cormorants, gulls and other sea birds. Day trips leave
from Pisco harbour at 07:00 daily.

Tambo Colorado *

In the valley of the Río Pisco, 46km (30 miles) east
of Pisco, this pre-Inca relic takes its name (*colorado*

TOUGH PLANTS

Few plants can survive the harsh environment of the highest areas of the Alto Plano – a wilderness of shattered rock, thin soil and bitter cold. One exception is the yareta plant, a bright green, spongy-looking succulent which huddles in the shelter of scattered boulders and grows only higher than 4500m (14,765ft) above sea level. Steeped in water for several days, its leaves are said to alleviate the symptoms of rheumatism and arthritis.

Opposite: *The Humming-bird, one of the Nazca symbols, seen from the air.*
Below: *A mummy at Ica Regional Museum.*

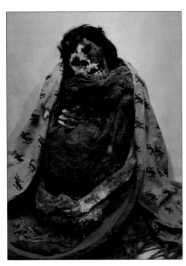

meaning 'red') from the painted mud-brick walls of its crumbling buildings. Open daily, 08:00–16:00.

Ica *

The provincial capital is an unassuming small city with no outstanding attractions. For those with time to kill between buses on the way from Lima to Nazca and points south, the **Regional Museum** (Ayabaca, open 08:00–19:00 Monday to Friday and 09:00–18:00 week-ends) has a surprisingly good collection of **Inca** and **Nazca** finds from local sites, including delicate feather cloaks and weavings, desiccated mummies, and also some Nazca pottery.

Nazca *

The small town of Nazca would not be on the tourist map of Peru but for its proximity to the fascinating Nazca Lines, in the **Pampa de Nazca** desert just outside town. A small airport is the base for flights over the Lines and there are hotels in all categories for those staying overnight.

Nazca Lines ***

The Nazca Lines comprise a maze of furrows around 20cm (8in) deep which are ploughed into the dry soil of the plains of San José, an area of desert 20km (15 miles) north of Nazca. With near-zero rainfall, the lines have, amazingly, survived intact for some 2600 years, although they were partially buried until the Peruvian archaeologist **Max Uhle** began the process of rediscovery in 1901. Uhle's work was taken over in the 1930s by the American archaeologist **Paul Kosok**, then by the German mathematician **Maria Reiche**, who spent five decades clearing the geometric patterns and animal figures that cover the flat, arid landscape. Declared a UNESCO World Heritage Site in 1994, the

Lines are a mixture of long, straight ruts and figures of animals including a hummingbird, a monkey and a fish, some of which are almost 500m (1640ft) long. From ground level, the Lines are impressive enough but it is hard to make out the outlines of these huge figures. From a light aircraft, however, the patterns are immediately obvious. There is much speculation as to how – and why – the lines were made, ranging from the sensationalist **Erich von**

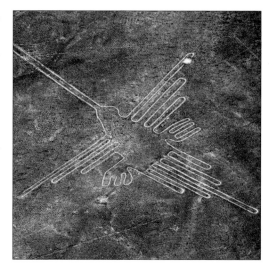

Daniken's claim in the 1970s that they were evidence of contact between the Nazca and visitors from space to more sober hypotheses that they were a form of astronomical calendar.

Museo Maria Reiche *

This is not so much a museum, but more a memorial to Maria Reiche (see panel, page 78) and her obsession with revealing the secrets of the lines, to which she devoted most of her life. Her tomb is in the garden of the museum (her former home) which is filled with her drawings and mathematical instruments. Pan-American Highway Kilometre 448, open daily 08:30–17:30.

Cantayoc Aqueducts *

The underground Cantayoc Aqueducts, 5km (3 miles) east of Nazca, are more properly qanats – a system of underground channels bringing water from the hills to irrigate desert land and indicating that the Nazca had independently discovered a technique that was also known in ancient Persia. The channels are still in use today, and it is possible to enter them (open 24 hours).

HOT AIR?

American businessman Jim Woodman visited the Nazca Lines in 1973 and became convinced that the Nazca intended their work to be seen from the air – and that they were capable of building hot-air balloons in which to soar above the desert. In 1975, Woodman test-flew a balloon inspired by images on Nazca pottery and textiles and built using only methods and techniques that would have been available to the ancient builders. Condor I successfully carried Woodman and a colleague to a height of 400m (1200ft) and stayed aloft for 14 minutes – proving at least that the Nazca could also have flown.

Above: *The vicuña is a shyer and wilder relative of the domesticated llama and alpaca and can be seen in several reserves in southern Peru.*

Cahuachi **

Often bypassed by visitors who make a beeline for the Lines, this collection of stone and mud-brick **stepped pyramids** is 25km (15 miles) west of Nazca. Next to the pyramids is a **cemetery** where the mummified bodies of Nazca nobles and rulers were interred, and also the ruins of a building used to prepare their cadavers for mummification. Those who have visited the pyramids and natron baths (mummification centres) of Egypt may find eerie similarities here, and it is not surprising that some more imaginative fantasists have suggested that the two ancient civilizations were somehow in communication. Cultural coincidence, however, is a more persuasive explanation.

Reserva Nacional Pampa Galeras **

The Pampa Galeras National Reserve, 90km (65 miles) east of Nazca, is a refuge for the endangered vicuña, and is one of the best places in Peru to see this slender, undomesticated relative of the llama and the alpaca in the wild. The reserve is not easily accessible without a four-wheel-drive vehicle, and is best visited on an organized tour from Nazca (*see* Tours and Excursions, page 93.)

AYACUCHO

Ayacucho province is Peru's **Quechua heartland**. In many ways, the region has lagged behind neighbouring areas, despite its apparently strategic central location in the south-central Andes, 583km (362 miles) southeast of Lima and 582km (362 miles) from Cuzco. Before the Inca, this was the base of the Huari civilization, the first Andean empire, which reached its zenith in the 6th century AD. However, unlike Cuzco, Ayacucho has missed out on the easy cash brought in by tourism, and in an area of few natural resources, poverty turned the province into fertile recruiting ground for the Sendero Luminoso during the 1980s and 1990s, leading to the imposition of martial law. With the Senderista conflict seemingly over, Ayacucho is once again visitable. The province has a scattering of **ancient sites**, but is more memorable for its gracious **colonial churches and cathedrals** and colourful **arts and crafts**.

Ayacucho City
Boasting more than 30 beautiful colonial churches, Ayacucho – 2746m (9006ft) above sea level – is one of the richest centres of Hispanic heritage in Peru. It is also known as a centre of excellence for arts and crafts, and the **Santa Ana** quarter, ten minutes from the city centre, is home to families of weavers and potters.

Ayacucho's central square, the **Plaza de Armas**, is surrounded by some outstanding colonial buildings, including the **Consejo Municipal** (Town Hall), the **Prefectura** (Prefecture), and the magnificent **Palacio del Marques**, dating from 1550. Most of these now house local government offices and are not open to the public, but the splendid **Cathedral**, on the east side of the square, is not to be missed.

Cathedral ***
This lavish 17th-century edifice is the location of the **Museum of Religious Art**. Representations of native animals (including llamas) in the rich carvings and paintings that adorn the outside and interior of the building are evidence of local influ-

> **VICUÑAS**
>
> *Chaccu* – annual shearing – takes place in late May and early June. The vicuña has been driven close to extinction by being hunted for its valuable fleece. Shy and, unlike the llama and alpaca, apparently impossible to domesticate, it is easier to shoot than round up.

Below: *The Plaza de Armas is the heart of the old city of Ayacucho in the foothills of the Andes.*

ence on the opulent Spanish Baroque style of the Cathedral's architecture.

Other Colonial Churches

Few visitors will want to visit more than one or two of Ayacucho's treasury of churches, which all share a common style of architecture. Those which are worth a look include the churches of **La Compañía** at the corner of San Martín and 28 de Julio (next door to the Centro Cultural San Cristóbal); **San Juan de Dios**, at the corner of 28 de Julio and Itana; and **Santa Clara**, at the corner of Grau and Nazareno. A full list of Ayacucho's churches, and their opening times (which change unpredictably), is available from the tourist information office (*see* Tours and Excursions, page 93).

Below: *Spiny cacti, adapted to survive the arid environment, are among the few plants that flourish in southern Peru's semi-desert landscapes.*

Museum of Popular Art ★★

This museum has an excellent collection of local handicrafts including the famous *retablos* – wooden boxes of varying sizes crammed with colourful three-dimensional nativity scenes or depictions of local life. Located at Portal Union 28, it is open 10:15–17:30 Tuesday–Friday and 09:45–12:15 Saturday.

Centro Turistico Cultural San Cristóbal ★

Art galleries, craft shops, and several places to eat and drink make this cultural centre-cum-tourist mall a pleasant place to browse and hang out. At 28 de Julio 178, it is open from 10:00 until late.

Huari ★

Some 22km (13 miles) northeast of Ayacucho, the ancient capital of the pre-Inca Huari culture covers an area of about 2000ha (4940 acres). However, the hilltop site is less impressive than its Inca rivals – little excavation or restoration work has been carried out and many of the crumbling walls are overgrown with brush and cactus. It is open 08:00–17:30 daily.

Quinua **

Quinua, 37km (22 miles) northeast of Ayacucho and 14km (9 miles) from Huari, is noted for its skilled **potters**, who are said to be direct descendants of the Huari. Their work is on sale in numerous shops around this pretty village, which also has a small museum (open 10:00–16:30 daily) dedicated to Peru's struggle for independence from Spain.

Above: *Woven rugs and blankets can be found in Ayacucho's markets.*

Pampas de Ayacucho Historical Sanctuary *

Peruvians are fiercely patriotic and the location of the **Battle of Ayacucho**, which on 9 December 1824 represented the final defeat of the Spanish Empire in South America, is a national monument. The battlefield is marked by a stone obelisk but the site is of only marginal interest to anyone except a military historian with an interest in South American affairs.

Vilcashuamán *

This archaeological site 120km (47 miles) southeast of Ayacucho is 3470m (11,385ft) above sea level and was the communications hub of the Inca Empire, where two great Inca highways crossed. Little remains of its great temples and courtyards, except for a carved stone throne atop an ancient stone pyramid.

AYACUCHO CRAFTS

Woven rugs and blankets dyed with vegetable dyes, figurines carved from local alabaster, and the wooden boxes known as *retablos*, carved and painted with religious and traditional scenes, are typical of the arts and crafts to be found in the markets of Ayacucho province. All represent a fusion of post-Conquest Spanish influences with the centuries-old artistic traditions of the Quechua people.

APURIMAC

Apurimac province is well off the beaten track. Over-shadowed by the legendary Inca sites and natural wonders of more accessible provinces, Apurimac's main attractions are natural rather than man-made. The 5228m (16,000ft) summit of **Ampay** – only about 10km (6 miles) from the provincial capital, Abancay – lures alpine climbers and high-counter trekkers. On the slopes of the mountain, the 3635ha (8982-acre) **Ampay National Sanctuary** shelters a variety of rare and colourful bird species including the spectacular Andean cock-of-the-rocks.

AREQUIPA

Arequipa province is a region of wild contrasts, from the tranquil cloisters of Arequipa's **colonial churches and convents** to the wild landscapes of the **canyon country** and the snow-capped cones of towering **volcanoes**. In the Andagua region, the Valley of the Volcanoes is a spectacular region of dormant volcanic cones; volcanic activity has endowed the province with hot springs and rock that is easy to shape into magnificent buildings or awesome canyonside terraces, but also brings a legacy of seismic activity that has repeatedly rocked its towns and villages – most recently in 2001.

The Coast

Arequipa's coastal plain is near-desert, with a rocky coastline interspersed with impressive sand dunes. Few places along this barren shore merit a stopover, but the small town of **Camaná**, 133km (90 miles) southwest of

TOMB RAIDERS

Tomb raiders, known as *hua-queros*, have looted much of Peru's rich cultural heritage over centuries. During the colonial era, the Spanish authorities actually issued licences to loot the mud-brick pyramids of northern sites such as Batan Grande, near Chiclayo. Hundreds of thousands of pits, up to 10m (33ft) across, pockmark the ancient temple sites such as Sicán and Chan Chan – some of them dug as recently as the 1970s. In 1604, Spanish *huaqueros* even diverted the Moche River to wash away most of the Huaca del Sol temple mound to reveal its treasures, which were looted and melted down.

Arequipa, has sandy beaches around 5km (3 miles) south of town. From Camaná, the main road loops inland to Arequipa and the stretch of coastline between Camaná and the small port of **Mollendo** is virtually trackless wilderness. Mollendo, which grew up as the seaport serving Arequipa and its silver mines, is connected to the city by a desert highway and a (freight-only) railway and is a possible stopover for those heading south along the coast to Tacna province and on to Chile. Now a sleepy backwater (except when weekenders from Arequipa are drawn to its huge beach and the nearby resort of **Mejia** in the warmer months between January and March), Mollendo has a number of budget and mid-range hotels but no big resort hotels.

The **Mejia Lagoons National Reserve**, 6km (4 miles) south of Mollendo, comprises an area of dunes and

SPONDYLUS SHELLS

The shells of the spondylus, a conch-like shellfish up to 20cm (8in) in length, were highly valued by all the pre-Columbian cultures of Peru and have been found in ancient tombs all over the country. Hoards of the shells were buried with the Lords of Sicán and Sipán in the north, and ornately carved spondylus shells can be seen in the National Anthropological, Archaeological and Historical Museum in Lima. Spondylus do not live in Peruvian waters, so the shells (imported from Ecuador) had rarity value and may have been used as currency.

Opposite: *Arequipa has the best preserved array of colonial-era buildings in southern Peru.*
Left: *Colonial arcades and palm trees on the Plaza de Armas, Arequipa.*

CHICHA

Chicha, Peru's ubiquitous traditional alcoholic beverage, was made by many of the ancient Peruvian cultures and played an important part in religious ceremonies. Today, it is still made for everyday use and special occasions, and almost every household has its own recipe. The basic ingredients are milled corn, natural yeasts, raw cane sugar, and flavourings such as canella and apple. *Chicha* takes about five days to ferment, and goes on getting stronger for up to a month – by which time it has quite a kick.

shallow brackish coastal lagoons which draw large flocks of waterfowl and waders (it is open from sunrise to sunset daily).

Arequipa City ***

Arequipa is Peru's second largest city. Its nickname, the 'White City', derives from its many imposing colonial churches and mansions, built from sillar, a pale volcanic rock. The city's location, beneath the three huge volcanic cones of **Misti** (5822m/19,092ft), **Chachani** (6075m/19,932ft) and **Pichu Pichu** (5571m/18,278ft) is breathtaking, and the city's wealth of historic buildings earned it UNESCO World Heritage status in 2000. The hub of historic Arequipa, as in all Peruvian colonial cities, is the **Plaza de Armas**, with the splendid **Cathedral** on its north side. Despite repeated natural disasters including earthquakes in 1868 and 2001, these magnificent edifices have stood the test of time.

Below: *Arequipa's Cathedral is one of the historic buildings that gives Peru's 'White City' its nickname.*

Cathedral ***

Founded in 1656, the Cathedral was destroyed by fire in 1844. Not long after being rebuilt, it was again demolished by the earthquake of 1868. Rebuilt, it was severely damaged by the 2001 earthquake, but has once again been reconstructed. Within, the cathedral is much less dark and ornate than most of Peru's great churches, with twelve marble columns symbolizing the Twelve Apostles. At Plaza de Armas, it is open daily 07:00–10:00 and 17:00–19:00.

Church of La Compañía **

This Jesuit church is a fine example of the elaborate Churrigueresque style (*see* panel, page 38), a uniquely Peruvian blend of Spanish Baroque influences and native stoneworking and woodworking skills and traditions. Located at Plaza de Armas, it is open daily 10:00–12:00 and 17:00–19:00.

Monasterio de Santa Catalina ★★★

This 'city within a city' dates from 1580, when it was founded by a wealthy widow, **Maria de Guzman**. The nunnery closed its doors to the outside world until 1970, when it was opened to visitors for the first time.

The convent complex covers about 20,000m² (23,920 sq yd) of cloisters, chapels, courtyards and cells linked by narrow alleys and stairways and takes one to two hours to explore fully. At Santa Catalina 300, it is open 09:00–16:00 daily.

Above: *Santa Catalina Convent is painted in vivid colours.*

Andean Sanctuaries Museum ★★★

This museum's centrepiece is the 'Lady of Ampato', also nicknamed 'Juanita' or 'the Ice Princess'. This mummified body of an adolescent girl dates from the Inca era and – along with many other such remains – is believed to indicate that the Inca had a taste for human sacrifice.

The mummy was discovered by Peruvian climber **Migeul Zárate** and archaeologist **Johan Reinhardt** near the peak of the 6288m (20,631ft) Ampato mountain, after a volcanic eruption melted the layer of snow and ice that had preserved its ceremonial tomb for more than five centuries. The Inca are believed to have made such mountain-top sacrifices to appease their deities and avert natural disasters. The museum, at Santa Catalina 210, is open 09:00–17:45 Monday–Saturday, closed Sunday; the Juanita mummy is on show only May–December.

LUPIN SEEDS

Most Peruvian village farmers rotate their staple crops, planting various kinds of potato, corn, and beans at different seasons. One staple crop is the lupin, with its colourful flowers and bean-like seed pods. Lupin seeds are highly nutritious, but making them edible is a labour-intensive process – they must first be boiled, then soaked in clean water and rinsed repeatedly over several days.

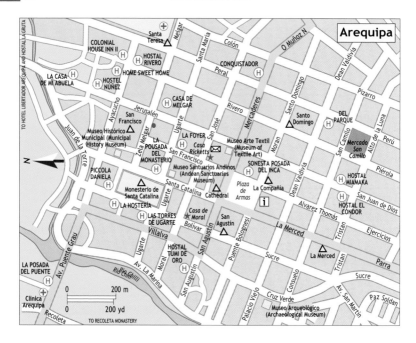

Arequipa

MUD BRICKS

On the outskirts of most Peruvian towns and cities – usually near river beds that provide mud or clay – are primitive-looking structures that might almost be taken for ancient temples. These are brick kilns, where mud mixed with straw is baked into weather-resistant bricks. In Peru's mostly arid climate, mud-brick buildings last for years; their thick walls stay cool in the daytime and radiate heat at night. Most houses are unpainted, though some people paint just the front wall of their home, usually in green, blue, pink or white.

Recoleta Monastery **

Founded by the Franciscan order in 1648, this church is most interesting for its collection of works by painters of the Cuzco School. It also houses a collection of Inca and other pre-Conquest relics. At La Recoleta 117, it is open 09:00–19:00 Monday–Saturday.

Other Museums *

Arequipa has a handful of other museums that are mainly of interest to specialists but are worth a short visit for those with time on their hands. The **Archaeological Museum** (Cruz Verde 303, open 09:30–13:00 Monday–Friday) displays finds from archaeological sites around the province, including weavings, pottery and jewellery. The **Municipal History Museum** (San Francisco 407, open 07:00–15:00 Monday–Friday) has a rather shabby collection of colonial-era prints, maps, and portraits that shed some light on Arequipa during the Spanish heyday and after independence. The **Museum of Textile Art** (Mercaderes 141, open 10:00–20:30 Monday–Saturday) has exhibits of traditional weaving looms and other tools of the weaver's and dyer's trades. The museum also shows an interesting 12-minute video about Arequipa.

Colonial Mansions **

Arequipa's streets are lined with fine Baroque colonial buildings built with the easily worked volcanic stone called sillar, which gave the 'White City' its nickname. Many are still privately owned or are used as local government offices but two now house bank branches and are open to visitors. The **Casa de Moral** (Moral 318, open 09:00–17:00 Monday–Saturday, guided tours in English) also has an interesting collection of maps charting the exploration of Peru and the Andes; the **Casa Ricketts** (San Francisco 57, open 09:15–13:00 and 16:30–18:30 Monday–Friday; 09:30–12:00 Sunday), was a bishop's palace, then an opulent private home and has fine carved fountains in its courtyard and an elaborately carved gateway. Away from the town centre, at Huasacache (9km/5.5 miles from central Arequipa) is one of the most lavish colonial mansions of all, the **Casa del Fundador** (Founder's House), 17th-century home of the founder of Arequipa, the Spanish aristocrat **Manuel García de Carbajal**.

Paucaparta *

This small village 8km (5 miles) from central Arequipa is worth a taxi ride just for the great views of Misti. It is surrounded by Inca terraces which are still cultivated

Above: *Buildings such as the Casa del Moral, built of white limestone, have earned Arequipa its nickname of the 'White City'.*

YUCCA PLANTS

Spindly yucca plants grow all over Peru and have many uses – planted close together, their spiny leaves make a useful hedge for penning in livestock, their fibres are used to make cord and rope, the fleshy stem is fried or boiled as a carbohydrate-rich foodstuff, and the sap and juice are credited with a variety of therapeutic uses.

CHURCH BALCONIES

In Ferreñafe, near Chiclayo, the church of **Santa Lucia** is an example of a colonial church with a balcony above the main door. Such balconies are typical of churches which had a large Indian congregation. On major holy days, there were too many celebrants to fit into the church – hence the balcony, from which the priest could conduct mass to a congregation gathered in the plaza outside.

today and 2km (1 mile) from the village square with its pretty church is the historic **Sabandia Watermill** (open 09:00–17:00 Monday–Saturday), built in 1621 and restored in 1973.

Salinas and Aguada Blanca National Reserve *

This natural reserve 35km (22 miles) east of Arequipa surrounds a salt lake which attracts migratory flamingoes and other wading birds during the rainy season. In the dry season, from May to December, it becomes a dry salt pan that shimmers with mirages under the hot sun.

THE CANYON COUNTRY
Colca Canyon ***

Formed by the Colca River as it carves its way through soft volcanic rock to the Pacific Ocean, the Colca Canyon (164km/131 miles northwest of Arequipa) is 3400m (11,512ft) deep. Its sides are an amazing man-made landscape of hundreds of terraces built long before the Spanish conquest and still farmed today. The towns and villages of the valley – Chivay, Pampamarca, Callata, Cabanaconde, Callalli, Sibayo, Ichupampa, and Yanque – preserve a traditional way of life, with colourful religious festivals, folk art, music and dance. Chivay, 3660m (12,008ft) above sea level, and Canaconde are the best bases for exploring the region, with a choice of mid-range and budget places to stay. The **Cruz del Condor** lookout offers magnificent views of the canyon and the volcanic peaks of Ampato, Sabancaya and Hualca Hualca which overlook it.

Below: *The arid slopes and terraces of the Colca Canyon.*

Colca has become a focus for a wide range of adventure holidays, including riding, llama trekking, and whitewater rafting (best booked through specialist tour operators in Lima or Arequipa – *see* Tours and Excursions, page 93). The trek to the bottom of the canyon is demanding, taking at least four days, and those planning to do it

should allow extra time to allow for acclimatizing to the high altitude. Colca (and nearby Cotahuasi) are among the best places in Peru to see huge condors soaring majestically above the cliffs and terraces.

Above: *A condor soaring in the Colca Canyon, seen from the Cruz del Condor lookout point.*

Cotahuasi Canyon ***

Cotahuasi, at 3535m (11,598ft), is even deeper and more stunning than Colca and offers even more demanding trekking. Allow at least seven days to explore the canyon and its villages thoroughly: this is a trek that should be attempted only with a specialist walking operator.

The most picturesque villages in the Colca valley are **Cotahuasi** (2683m/8803ft above sea level), **Callata** and **Pampamarca**, and like the Colca Canyon there are opportunities for hiking, rafting, mountain biking and even paragliding. **Luicho** village is noted for its hot springs, and one of the valley's most spectacular sights is the 250m (492ft) waterfall at **Sipia**.

El Misti *

Despite its imposing height, El Misti is a relatively easy mountain to climb for experienced and fit mountain walkers. That said, the ascent is physically challenging and should not be attempted without a guide and the proper equipment, including crampons. The easiest ascent is from the 4000m (13,124ft) contour, which can

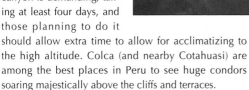

COLCA VALLEY FESTIVALS

15 May: **San Isidro Labrador**, Corporaque
13 June: **San Antonio de Padua**, Callalli
24 June: **San Juan Bautista**, Ichupampa and Sibayo
15 August: **Virgen de la Asuncion** (Assumption), Chivay
16 August: **Virgen del Carmen**, Cabanaconde
8 December: **Virgen de la Concepcion**, Yanque

Right: *The cone of El Misti, a dormant volcano, dominates the skyline of Arequipa.*

be reached by hired four-wheel-drive vehicle. Specialist walking and climbing agencies in Arequipa and Lima can arrange guides and transport.

Toro Muerto Stone Carvings **

The petroglyphs of Toro Muerto, 100km (64 miles) north of Camaná, are an astonishing assortment of volcanic boulders, scattered across some two square kilometres of semidesert near the town of Corire and carved with outlines of mythical beasts, birds and human figures. Estimated to be around 1000 years old, they are attributed to the Huari culture.

MOQUEGUA AND TACNA

Peru's two southernmost provinces are surprisingly different, though neither is of much interest except to those travelling onward into Chile. There is little to detain the traveller in Moquegua, a semidesert region which was largely spurned by Peru's ancient civilizations and would have remained unsettled but for the discovery of copper, which became a major export for Peru during the 9th century. Moquegua, the eponymous provincial capital, is a dusty and dilapidated town. Ilo, the provincial seaport 95km (60 miles) west of the capital, is equally uninteresting.

Tacna province, bordering Chile, is more prosperous and more fertile. Between the arid coastlands and sierras that rise to heights of more than 5500m (18,045ft) is a fertile zone with a near-Mediterranean climate that allows vines, olives and avocados to flourish.

Tacna City

Despite its remoteness from the capital (1300km/830 miles), 19th-century Tacna city was a boom town at the heart of the lucrative nitrate mining industry that provoked the 'Pacific War' between Peru (and its ally Bolivia) and Chile (*see* Historical Calendar, page 17). After Peru's defeat, Tacna city was occupied by Chile until 1929 when the border between the two countries, 36km (22 miles) south of Tacna, was finally settled by treaty. The legacy of its 19th- and early 20th-century prosperity includes a **Cathedral** and a **monumental fountain**, both designed by **Gustav Eiffel**, creator of the Eiffel Tower in Paris, and a **Railway Museum** (in the railway station, open 08:00–17:30 daily) with a remarkable collection of mainly British-built steam locomotives. The railway line that links Tacna with Arica in Chile is another relic of the nitrate boom.

CHINESE RESTAURANTS

Chinese or *chifa* restaurants can be found almost everywhere in Peru, though they are more common in the big cities of the coast. Their owners are descendants of immigrants from China's Canton (Guangzhou) region, who began to arrive in numbers in the 1840s. More than 90,000 Chinese people came to Peru during the 19th century, as agricultural workers and domestic servants, and many of their descendants went into the restaurant business. The menu is usually a fusion of Peruvian ingredients and Chinese cooking styles – very different from Cantonese cooking in Hong Kong or Guangzhou today.

Left: *Petroglyphs of San Francisco de Miculla, located 22km (14 miles) from Tacna.*

Southern Peru at a Glance

Southern coastal regions are hot and dry year round, with virtually no rain, but morning ground fog may obscure the Nazca Lines and strong after-noon breezes can make boat trips in the Paracas reserve uncomfortable. The dry season in Apurimac is from late May until Sep, with frequent rain and snow on Andean slopes from Jan until Apr. The best time for trekking the Colca and Cotahuasi Canyons is Apr–Nov. The canyon region is cool all year, with chilly nights.

By road: The Pan-American Highway links Pisco, Ica, Nazca, Camaná, Arequipa, Moquegua and Tacna with Lima; a major highway con-nects Ayacucho with Pisco (around 320km/200 miles). Main roads connect Abancay with Cuzco (200km/130 miles) and Arequipa with Juliaca (320km/200 miles) in Puno province. The Pan-American Highway crosses into Chile at the border town of Concordia, 36 km (22 miles) south of Tacna.
By air: Daily flights from Lima to Ica, Nazca, Ayacucho, Arequipa and Tacna.

Buses operate between major towns; the usual assortment of *colectivos*, shared taxis and taxis operate in and around larger towns. For journeys into the canyon country, El Misti and the national reserves, specialist tour agencies in Arequipa arrange vehicles and drivers for groups of all sizes.

There are few if any luxury hotels in southern Peru, but the region's main hubs are well supplied with mid-range and budget places to stay.

Ayacucho
MID-RANGE
Ayacucho Hotel Plaza, 9 de Diciembre 184, tel: 81 22 02, fax 81 23 14. An attractive colonial exterior conceals rather dull but adequately equipped rooms, some with balconies. This is the best accommodation Ayacucho has to offer (but at a mid-level price).

BUDGET
Hotel Santa Rosa, Lima 166, tel: 81 46 14, fax: 81 20 83. Amiable small hotel in the centre of town with largish rooms, en-suite hot showers, courtyard and roof terrace and a decent restaurant.

Pisco
MID-RANGE
Embassy Beach Hotel, San Martín 1119, tel: 84 26 26 99. Close to the beach, this is the best place to stay in Pisco, with comfortable, well-equipped rooms (satelllite TV, minbar, etc.) and an excellent restaurant.

BUDGET
Posada Hispana, Calle Bolognese 22, tel: 53 63 63, www.posadahispana.com Friendly, with multilingual staff, good rooms, and a very pleasant café-terrace.

Nazca
LUXURY
Nazca Lines Hotel, Jirón Bolognesi, tel: 52 22 93, fax: 52 21 12. Despite its name, this hotel is in the centre of Nazca town. Smart rooms, good facilities including an open-air pool. The hotel offers tours to the Lines and other sights around Nazca.
Hotel Cantayo, Cantayoc, tel: 52 22 64, e-mail: hotel cantayo@amauta.rcp.net.pe Great location, lavish grounds (enclosing a large open-air pool). Near the famous aqueducts of Cantayoc.

MID-RANGE
Nido del Condor, Nazca Airport, tel: 52 24 24, e-mail: acnasca@terra.com.pe Motel-style with a small pool, next to the airport. Ideal for those flying in for an early-morning flight over the Lines before travelling on.

BUDGET
Hotel el Mirador de Nazca, Plaza de Armas, tel: 52 3121, fax: 52 37 41. More of the faded grandeur that Peru does so well; rooms have en-suite bathrooms. Central location on the main square.

Southern Peru at a Glance

Arequipa

LUXURY

Hotel Libertador Arequipa,
Plaza Bolivar, Selva Alegre, tel:
21 51 10, www.libertador.
com.pe Managed by one of
Peru's top hotel chains, this is
the best (and most expensive)
hotel in Arequipa and the
South. Quiet location 1.5km
(1 mile) from the city centre,
extensive grounds, a pool and
other luxury facilities; the best
hotel restaurant in Arequipa.
Sonesta Posada del Inca,
Portal de Flores 116, tel: 21
55 30, www.sonesta.com
All the facilities including
gym and rooftop pool. Ask for
a room overlooking the
Cathedral (but expect to pay a
hefty surcharge for the view
in high season). Good value.

MID-RANGE

Hostal La Gruta, La Gruta
304, Selva Alegre, tel: 22 46
31, www.lagruta.com Small,
quiet hotel with garden and
well-equipped rooms, about
1.6km (1 mile) from the centre. Airport shuttle available.

BUDGET

Casa de Melgar, Melgar 108A,
tel/fax: 22 24 59, www.lacasa
demelgar.com A great place to
stay; comfortable modern
rooms in an 18th-century
building with a quiet inner
courtyard and café-restaurant.

WHERE TO EAT

Ayacucho and Arequipa are
the only spots that have

restaurants that stand out from
the crowd. Even here, there
are no luxury restaurants and
it is hard to spend more than
around $15 on a slap-up meal.

Ayacucho

BUDGET

Soncollay, Portal San
Agustin 149, tel: 56 81 84.
Above the Plaza de Armas;
has great views and serves
traditional dishes such as
grilled guinea-pig and alpaca.
Pizzeria Italiana, Belido 490.
Pasta dishes and pizza from the
wood oven. Pleasant and cosy.

Arequipa

MID-RANGE

Picanteria Los Guisos,
Lambramani 111, tel: 46 44
53. Cavernous hacienda-style
restaurant 2km (1.2 miles)
from the city centre (a five-
minute taxi ride) with a good
choice of local and regional
Peruvian dishes, outdoor
tables, and the inevitable
ensemble of folk musicians.
Tradicion Arequipena, Av.
Dolores 111, tel: 42 64 67.
Best restaurant in Arequipa;
2km (1.2 miles) from centre
and well worth the taxi ride.
Regional cuisine and a 'magic
garden' where musicians and
performers entertain diners.

BUDGET

Mixtos, Pasaje Catedral 115,
tel: 20 53 43. Seafood, pizza
and Peruvian dishes. Open-
air tables, central location off
the Plaza de Armas.

TOURS AND EXCURSIONS

Nazca Lines overflights from
Nazca's aerodrome between
08:00 and 10:00 and again in
early afternoon, depending
on visibility and wind conditions. Flights last 30 mins and
cost US$35–US$50. The main
company is **Aerocondor**, tel:
(056) 52 24 24, www.aero
condor.com.pe, which also
operates more expensive flights
over the Nazca Lines from Ica
(Las Dunas Sun Resort, Av. La
Angostura 400, Ica, tel: (056)
25 62 30), costing US$150.
Balegra Tours, Hotel Alegria,
Jr Lima 168 Nazca, tel: 52 24
44, www.nazcaperu.com
Nazca Lines flights, tours to
Ica, Paraca, Islas Ballestas.
Mystery Peru, Ignacio Morse-
sky 124, Nazca, tel: (056) 52
23 79, www.mysteryperu.com
Tours of Pampa Galeras, also
Paracas National Reserve, the
Ica desert, Nazca Lines.
AI Travel and Tours, Arequipa,
tel: (054) 22 20 52, www.
aitraveltours.com Colca Can-
yon, other tours from Arequipa.
Specialist tours to the canyon
country and the Cruz del
Condor: **Colonial Tours**,
Santa Catalina 106, Arequipa,
tel: (054) 28 68 68 e-mail:
colonialtours02@hotmail.com
Illary Tours, Santa Catalina
205, Arequipa, tel: (054) 22
08 44, e-mail: illarytouraqp@
latinmail.com www.illary.pe
**Ayacucho Tourist
Information Office**, Plaza de
Armas, Ayacucho,
tel: 81 25 48.

6
Northern Peru

Peru's northern provinces, stretching from Lima to the border with Ecuador in the north, have for many years been overshadowed by the country's better-known attractions.

Yet this region of arid coastal plains wedged between the sea and the Andean cordillera is one of the most fascinating in the entire country, with **colonial cities** such as Trujillo, **archaeological sites** that rival Machu Picchu but are far less overrun with visitors, and Peru's only world-class **palm-fringed beaches**, on the southern shore of the Gulf of Guayaquil.

North of Lima, the **Cordillera Blanca** mountain range rises to the summit of **Huascarán**, 6768m (22,205ft) above sea level. The highest peak in Peru, Huascarán is capped with snow and surrounded by lakes and glaciers. The Cordillera Blanca merges with the **Cordillera Huayhuash**, rising to its highest at **Yerupaja**, at 6634m (21,766ft) the country's second highest peak. **Chiquian**, 3200m (10,499 ft) above sea level, is the starting point for the ascent of Yerupaja, generally rated as the most challenging technical climb in the Peruvian Andes.

Nor is the north devoid of ancient relics. This was the heartland of three great civilizations, the **Chavín**, **Mochica** (Moche) and **Chimu** cultures, which pre-dated the Inca and have left impressive remains. Near Trujillo, the mud-brick metropolis of **Chan Chan** is one of Peru's most fascinating lost cities, and the hub of an empire that flourished long before the Incas. The relics

DON'T MISS

*** Chan Chan: enormous, ancient metropolis of adobe brick.
*** Sipán: stunning archaeological finds and a superb new museum.
** Trujillo: attractive colonial town.
** Huascarán National Park: awesome glacier scenery surrounds Peru's highest peaks.

Opposite: *The massive mud-brick walls of the Huaca del Dragón.*

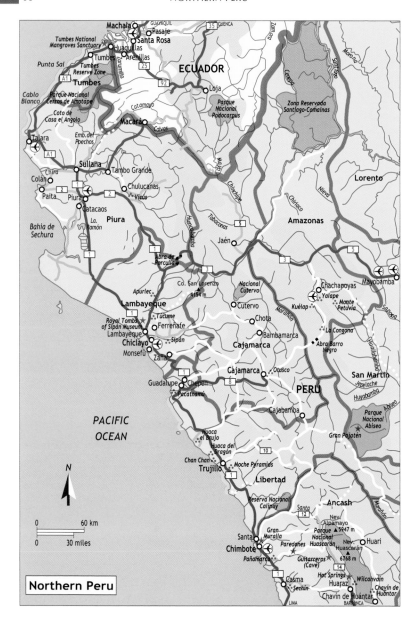

Northern Peru

of the **Lords of Sipán** rank as world-class treasures, and there are other archaeological sites at **Chavín**, **Yayno**, **Sechin** and **Túcume**, with its complex of adobe pyramids that have survived for more than 1300 years. In the northern highlands, the city of **Cajamarca** was a northern hub of the Inca Empire, prized for its hot springs, and is known as Peru's 'carnival capital' because of the colourful parades and bands that take place here in February and March.

All the region's major towns are on, or near, the coast and the Pan-American Highway links the northern coastal cities with Lima, passing through the dull modern port city of **Chimbote** on the way to the more interesting colonial capital of **Trujillo**, gateway to the north.

With Cuzco, Machu Picchu and the Inca Trail now so overloaded with tourists that the Peruvian government has been forced to limit visitor numbers, and with a waiting list of up to two months to walk the Inca Trail, northern Peru is likely to come into its own as visitors seek alternative sights and activities.

HUASCARÁN NATIONAL PARK

The Huascarán National Park, in the heart of the Cordillera Blanca, covers 340,000ha (840 sq miles) and comprises almost 300 clear, ice-cold mountain lakes and 663 glaciers on the slopes and summits of Peru's highest mountains. Listed since 1985 as a UNESCO World Natural Heritage Site, it includes protected areas for unique Andean vegetation such as the quenual tree, and birds and animals including the Andean condor and the vicuña. The town of **Huaraz** is the gateway to the park, with a wide choice of places to stay and eat and a number of specialist tour agencies which

WATER ISSUES

The rivers that flow out of the Andean cordillera to the Pacific are vital to the cities, industry and agriculture of the arid coast. But water is by no means an unlimited resource. In Lima, poor long-term planning means there is a conflict between the requirements of the national electricity supplier, which needs to pen up rivers behind its dams to generate the capital's electricity supply, and the water authority, which needs to release the same watercourses to supply water to homes, farms and businesses. Elsewhere, there is a clash between mining companies, which abstract huge quantities of water from lakes and rivers, and local communities and farmers.

Below: *The snow-capped summit of Mt Huascarán in the heart of one of Peru's most awe-inspiring national parks.*

arrange trips and treks to the park's highlights, including the **Pastoruri Glacier**, **Lake Llanganuco** at the foot of Mount Huascarán, and the thermal springs of **Monterrey**, just outside Huaraz.

CHAVÍN DE HUÁNTAR

Southeast of Huaraz, the eerie archaeological complex of Chavín de Huántar stands on a chilly, windswept site 3180m (10,434ft) above sea level. Built around 1200BC, this labyrinth of tunnels, temples and stone buildings was the ceremonial heart of one of Peru's earliest empires, the Chavín culture.

In a tunnel beneath the principal temple, a fearsome 4.5m (15ft) monolith, the *Lanzon*, represents one of the deities of this long-lost civilization. The ruins are 1km (0.6 miles) south of the modern village of Chavín and are open 08:00–16:00 daily.

Below: *The streets of Trujillo, the largest city in northern Peru, display a wealth of colourful colonial architecture.*

TRUJILLO

Trujillo, Peru's third largest city with a population of around 650,000, is the capital of La Libertad province and the only large city in the north. On the coast 561km (349 miles) north of Lima, it lies at the mouth of the Moche valley, cradle of the Mochica and Chimu civilizations (*see* page 16), which flourished between 200BC and AD700, leaving a remarkable legacy of ruins, pottery and gold and silver jewellery. Founded by the conquistador **Martin de Estete** – who, like his commander Pizarro, came from the Spanish city of Trujillo and named his new city after his home town – Trujillo was a flourishing colonial seaport, and was surrounded by ramparts to protect it from pirate raids. After Independence, it became even wealthier, conducting a prosperous trade in sugar and raw cotton from the plantations of the fertile hinterland.

Those decades of prosperity endowed Trujillo with a rich legacy of colonial architecture, and it is undoubtedly the most picturesque city in northern Peru. Its year-round sunny climate has earned it the nickname 'city of eternal spring,' and the nearby beaches – **Delicias**, **Salaverry**, **Huanchaco** and **Chicama** – are popular seaside getaways for Peruvians and also attract surfers from all over the world. The city is noted as the capital of the **marinera**, one of Peru's best-loved traditional dances, and for the reed canoes known as *caballitos de totora* which have been made to the same design for thousands of years and are still in use by local fishermen.

A striking **Cathedral**, dating from 1647, stands on Trujillo's Plaza de Armas and other striking colonial buildings include the **Iturregui Palace**, dating from the early 19th century; the **Casa de Los Leones**, a fine mansion which now houses the tourist police office; and the **Casona Orbegoso**, a private museum with a collection of colonial furniture, paintings and sculpture. Trujillo's most interesting **historic sights**, however, lie a short distance from town and date from long before the colonial period.

Sun and Moon Temples ***

Some 8km (5 miles) south of the town centre, the Temples of the Sun and the Moon are the most impressive relics of the **Moche culture**. The Sun Temple is a ziggurat (stepped pyramid) rising in tiers to a height of 43m (141 ft). Approximately 500m (545yd) from the Sun Temple, the Temple of the Moon is a complex of buildings rising one on top of another. Dating from

Above: *The lavishly decorated dining room of the Casona Orbegoso, one of Trujillo's fine old colonial mansions.*

REED BOATS

The *caballitos* used by Huanchaco fishermen look just like those depicted on vases dating from as far back as 2500BC and are remarkably similar to those used on Lake Titicaca – and on the Nile, a similarity that prompted Thor Heyerdahl (*see* Ra Expedition, page 67) to surmise that ancient Egytians could have used a larger version to cross the Atlantic Ocean. The boats are made from totora reeds that grow in huge beds north of Huanchaco.

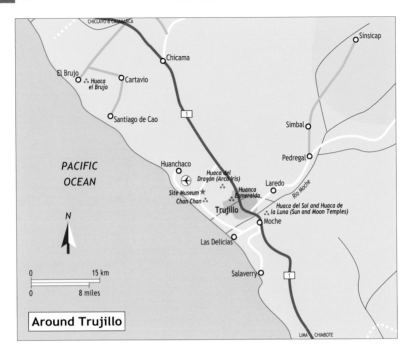

Around Trujillo

(Map labels) CHICLAYO & CAJAMARCA · Sinsicap · Chicama · El Brujo · Huaca el Brujo · Cartavio · Santiago de Cao · Simbal · Pedregal · PACIFIC OCEAN · Huanchaco · Huaca del Dragón (Arco Iris) · Laredo · Rio Moche · Site Museum · Chan Chan · Huanca Esmeralda · Trujillo · Huaca del Sol and Huaca de la Luna (Sun and Moon Temples) · Moche · N · Las Delicias · 0 15 km · 0 8 miles · Salaverry · LIMA CHIMBOTE

different eras of the Moche culture, their walls are adorned with multicoloured frescoes, the most dramatic of which depicts **Aja Paec**, the Moche god of fire. The complex is open 09:00–16:00 daily.

Chan Chan ★★★

The Trujillo region's most epic site is 5km (3 miles) northwest of Trujillo town centre, close to the sea. Chan Chan, the **City of the Sun**, is an amazing complex of mud-brick pyramids, plazas, warehouses and dwellings, sprawling across an area of 20km² (almost 8 sq miles). This was the capital of the **Chimu civilization** and the seat of its ruler, the **Chimu-Capac**. Before their empire was toppled and absorbed by the Inca (who cut the ingenious system of aqueducts that irrigated the surrounding arid land and brought water to Chan Chan, forcing the Chimu to surrender virtually without

---

ELDER TREES

Leafy, fast-growing elder trees are traditionally planted near peasant homes in rural northern Peru. Their white flowers, black berries and leaves are used in a variety of recipes and remedies; their most important medicinal use is in a tea which is given to women to aid recovery after childbirth.

a fight), the Chimu capital housed as many as 100,000 people. Archaeological research indicates that the Chimu at their zenith had a highly sophisticated civilization, capable of remarkable architecture and inventive agricultural techniques which allowed them to create fertile farmland from the unpromising semi-desert of the coast. They also made fine pottery and exquisite gold and silver filigree jewellery, examples of which can be seen in the **site museum**, outside the main entrance to Chan Chan.

Built between the 12th and 15th centuries, Chan Chan consists of nine major structures, from around 200m (660ft) to 400m (1300ft) in length and linked by a labyrinth of alleys, ramps and plazas. Because of the region's waterless climate, these adobe structures – the largest such complex in the Americas – are amazingly well preserved. Their massive walls are up to 4m (13ft) thick and are intricately decorated with astonishingly skilled reliefs of geometric patterns, symbols, animals, and mythological beings. The site is open 09:00–16:30 daily; the Chan Chan ticket gives admission to all the sites mentioned overleaf.

Huaca del Dragón ★★

Also known as the **Huaca del Arco Iris**, this Chimu sacred site lies 5km (3 miles) northwest of Trujillo. It is

> **LEGENDS OF CHAN CHAN**
>
> Legends surround the ruins of Chan Chan, telling of foreigners who have struck it lucky by discovering treasure-trove left by the ancient city's Chimu builders. Martin de Estete is said to have discovered a throne of gold inlaid with pearls, and in 1864 an American named Ephraim George Squier is claimed to have found a cache of silver goblets. Whether or not these stories are true, Chan Chan probably did contain fabulous treasures which have been looted and destroyed since its fall.

Below: *Stylized reliefs of sea birds and fishes adorn the labyrinthine walls of ancient Chan Chan.*

Below: *This mud brick frieze at Huaca del Dragón depicts an ancient Chimu deity.*

easy to see how it has earned its names: its walls are covered with elaborate, colourful friezes of mythological creatures and anthropomorphic figures which probably represent deities and demigods from the Chimu pantheon, some of which do indeed resemble dragons, and with coloured rainbow arches. The site is open 09:00–16:30 daily.

Huaca el Brujo **

This important temple site stands in the Chicama Valley, 34km (21 miles) northwest of Trujillo. A relic of the **Mochica culture**, it consists of three large ceremonial buildings of clay brick – **Huaca el Brujo**, **Huaca de Cao Viejo** which has walls covered with paintings and reliefs, and **Huaca Prieta**, the oldest and least well preserved of the three. Its builders are believed to have settled here as early as 3500BC, and over the next 1000 years developed from a simple hunter-gatherer society into a settled culture, farming beans, peppers, cotton and other crops in the valley and fishing in its streams and rivers. Open 09:00–16:30 daily.

Huanchaco *

This small fishing town is 12km (7 miles) northwest of Trujillo. Quieter than the regional capital, it is a convenient base for exploring the province and its attractions. Its beaches attract surfers, but the waves are too strong and the water too chilly for ordinary swimmers – a fact that has saved Huanchaco from being transformed from an old-fashioned fishing community into a full-scale holiday resort. Many fishermen still use the remarkable reed canoes known as *caballitos* ('little horses', *see* panel, page 99) which have been in use, virtually unchanged, for almost 4500 years.

CHICLAYO

Chiclayo, 210km (135 miles) north of Trujillo, is a bustling, modern city of around half a million people which owes its place on the tourist trail to the discovery in 1987 of the **royal Moche tombs of Sipán** (*see* below) – a find that ranks along with the

greatest archaeological discoveries of all time. Chiclayo has plenty of hotels and restaurants, and its enormous marketplace, the **Mercado Modelo**, is a sight worth seeing in its own right, with dozens of stalls selling straw hats and baskets, colourful woven bags and blankets, and a whole section devoted to healing herbs and charms. That said, few will want to linger here after visiting Sipán and the other nearby archaeological sites.

Above: *Fishermen at Huanchaco still use traditional boats known as* caballitos, *made from bundles of reeds that grow abundantly beside the nearby river mouth. Such boats have been used for thousands of years.*

Sipán (Huaca Rajada) ★★★

The unearthing of Sipán ranks along with the rediscovery of the tomb of Tutankhamun in Egypt or the royal tombs of Mycenae in Greece as one of the most exciting archaelogical finds of all time.

The tomb of the **Lord of Sipán** – a Moche aristocrat who had been buried along with all his earthly riches and the symbols of his high office – was discovered intact in 1987 by a Peruvian archaeological team led by **Dr Walter Alva**.

The Lord of Sipán died around AD230 and was interred wearing richly decorated robes and elaborate jewellery in gold, silver, turquoise and mother-of-pearl. Buried with him were members of his household, including three women, his bodyguards, a child and animals including two llamas and a dog – all, presumably, sacrificed in order to accompany their lord into the afterlife. Archaeologists have also discovered two more tombs, that of a former ruler of Sipán and of one of its high priests.

ANCIENT TRAILS

The best-known and most popular section of the Inca Trail, between Cuzco and Machu Picchu, is now seriously overcrowded and visitors are beginning to seek alternatives. In the stunning scenery around Cajamarca, the environmental conservation group APREC has opened up four routes following ancient trails through the stunning scenery of the Cajamarca Valley, with its lakes, mountain streams, Inca and pre-Inca relics. To find out more, visit the APREC website: www.aprec.org

El Clarin

Nearly 3m (10ft) in length, the *clarin* is a typical musical instrument of the Cajamarca region. It is made from cane, with a reed mouthpiece and a calabash cone, and its trumpet-like sound is heard on occasions such as Holy Week, Corpus Christi, and small-town saint's days. Also typical of the north are the *caja*, a small wooden drum, and the bamboo flute.

Cheap Guitars

Several towns around Peru, such as Namora in the Cajamarca region, are well known nationwide for the skills of their guitar-makers and other musical artisans. A top-quality handmade acoustic guitar will cost up to 1500 soles (around £300 or US$500), but guitar-makers also turn out cheap, virtually disposable guitars for festivals – these cost as little as 50 soles.

Lambayeque
Royal Tombs of Sipán Museum ★★★

Peru's newest museum was opened in 2002 at Lambayeque, some 15km (9 miles) north of Chiclayo. Designed by Peruvian architect **Celso Prado**, it is an impressive, ultramodern building with a floodlit, pyramidal exterior that is an effective introduction to the treasures that await within. This is a world-class museum that deserves far more attention than it gets.

The entrance hall features outstanding displays of delicate pottery, decorated with representations of Moche deities, flowers and crops, fish, animals and people, along with scale models that show what Sipán looked like in its heyday. On the first floor, the most gorgeous exhibits are the gold, silver and turquoise earrings dicovered on site; even more breathtaking, however, are the exact replicas of the Royal Tombs on the ground floor, complete with their dazzling jewels, ornaments and golden ceremonial breastplates. Open 09:00–17:00 Tuesday–Sunday.

Zaña ★

Close to the modern village of the same name, this colonial settlement was founded in 1563 and abandoned after being wrecked by a great flood in 1720. Its

Right: *The Museum of the Tombs of the Lords of Sipán at Lambayeque houses Peru's newest and most exciting collection of precious archaeological finds.*

deserted squares, arcades and crumbling churches, including the convent of **San Agustin** and the churches of **San Francisco** and **La Merced**, are gradually being swallowed up by the surrounding desert. Open 24 hours.

FERREÑAFE
National Museum of Sicán **
Opened in 2001, this museum (not to be confused with Sipán) displays relics of the Lambayeque culture, which existed at around the same time (AD750–1375) as the Chimu. These include the bodies of nobles and their retinues which were interred in deep tombs wearing golden masks and headpieces. The museum is located 18km (11 miles) northwest of Chiclayo and is open 09:00–18:00 Tuesday–Sunday.

Above: *A gilded mask of the Lord of Sipán is just one of the treasures unearthed from the tombs of the ancient rulers of northern Peru.*

Túcume *
Like so many sights in the north of Peru, Túcume deserves a wider reputation. Just off the Pan-American Highway, 32km (20 miles) north of Lambayeque, around 30 mud-brick pyramids cover an area of more than 80ha (200 acres). Like Sicán, this was a centre of the Lambayeque culture and, although no spectacular finds have been made here, the site itself gives a powerful impression of the sophistication and skill of this lost civilization.

PIURA AND TUMBES
Towards the Ecuadorean border, the southern shores of the **Gulf of Guyaquil**, with white sand beaches, palm trees and mangroves, make a welcome contrast to the bleak stretches of shoreline further south and the arid desert and semidesert scenery inland. With a climate that is warm and sunny all year round, these beaches attract Peruvian holiday-makers and surfers, but see

> ### CABALLOS DE PASO
>
> *Caballos de paso* – slim and highly strung horses trained to pace elegantly in competition – are prized in Peru, and the heartland of this aristocratic pastime is in the La Libertad region, around Trujillo. The typical *caballo de paso* is chestnut, black or palomino, with slender forelegs, stands around 16 hands high – and can command a price of around US$50,000. Riders wear a loose white shirt and trousers, black sash, high boots, striped poncho and straw sombrero, and use a traditional high saddle and boot-like leather stirrups.

Above: *The Cathedral, on the Plaza de Armas, is the most prominent landmark in the old part of Piura.*

surprisingly few international visitors.

The beaches begin north of Talara and are dotted along a stretch of more than 160km (100 miles) of coastline to Tumbes, the northernmost city in Peru, which is only 27km (16 miles) from the border with Ecuador. The beaches, and a handful of nature reserves, are the main reasons for visiting this part of the country.

North of Chiclayo, the highway skirts a vast area of uninhabited desert that gives way to greener, more fertile terrain north of the Río Piura.

Piura *

Although it is one of the oldest colonial towns in Peru – founded in 1532 at the very beginning of the Spanish conquest – Piura, on the banks of the Río Piura, is a pleasant but unexciting provincial capital. Look out for the grand **Cathedral**, on the north side of the Plaza de Armas, which was founded in 1588 but almost completely rebuilt in 1960. Also worth making time for is the **Museum of Vicus Gold** (Huánuco 893, open 09:00–17:00 Tuesday–Sunday), displaying some remarkable finds from the long vanished Vicus culture which flourished in the Piura valley around 2000 years ago.

There are good beaches either side of Piura. **Colan**, a few kilometres north of the small port town of Paita and 50km (31 miles) west of Piura, is a pleasant, low-key beach resort with small hotels and restaurants catering mainly to weekenders from Piura.

Talara *

On the fringes of the desert, Talara blots the landscape with its pipelines and oil refineries, and the derricks

---

FLOODS

Piura and Tumbes provinces are very vulnerable to floods caused by fluctuations in El Niño, when massive downpours in the highlands cause rivers to burst their banks, destroying roads, bridges and homes. Floods in 1983 wiped out almost all the province's agriculture and made hundreds of thousands homeless. The phenomenon recurred in 1992 and 1998, making travel in the region very difficult.

and pumps of Peru's richest oilfields are scattered across the hinterland between here and Tumbes. That said, the coast has a number of pleasant small beach resorts and fishing villages.

Cabo Blanco **

This fishing village 40km (25 miles) north of Talara has a 1km (0.6-mile) sandy beach that attracts surfers in winter with waves of up to 3m (10ft) high. It is also a noted game-fishing port, though prize black marlin are far rarer now than when Ernest Hemingway fished here in 1950. Tuna, dorado, barracuda and other game fish are also caught, and fully equipped boats can be hired by the day.

Máncora ***

Máncora, 69km (42 miles) south of Tumbes, is the north's most popular resort area and has the finest beaches in Peru, with some 20km (12 miles) of sand and surf stretching south from town.

Punta Sal **

Warm shallow water with an average temperature of 26°C (79°F) makes this small beach resort popular with those who find serious surf intimidating, including many weekenders from Tumbes. Punta Sal is 25km (15 miles) north of Máncora.

Tumbes

Tumbes is a charmless border town and its hot, humid climate encourages swarms of mosquitoes after dark. There is little of interest in town, which functions mainly as a

Below: *Palm trees, sand and warm water make Máncora on the Gulf of Guayaquil one of Peru's most attractive beach resorts.*

HAIRLESS DOGS

The hairless dogs of northern Peru are among the world's least attractive canines, with naked, wrinkled grey and pink skin and virtually no hair on their bodies. They do, however, have a long and honourable pedigree, dating back at least to the heyday of the Moche culture. They were revered as sacred to the moon deity, and may have been used in sacrificial rites.

stopover for travel to and from Ecuador. **Puerto Pizarro**, 16km (10 miles) to the north, is the gateway to a region of equatorial mangrove swamps and offshore islets such as the aptly named **Isla de Aves** (Isle of Birds) with its huge flocks of sea and forest birds, and **Isla de Amor**, which can be visited by boat.

Northwest Biosphere Reserve *

The Northwest Biosphere Reserve encompasses four wilderness regions that include a wide range of habitats, from coastal swamp to dry tropical woodland.

The **Tumbes National Mangroves Sanctuary** is a pocket of coastal wetland that protects Peru's only mangrove trees and can be explored by canoe with a guide. The **Cerros de Amotape National Park**, covering almost 1000km^2 (386 sq miles) of tropical forest, adjoins the **Coto de Caza el Angolo**, straddling the border with Piura province, and shelters wildlife that includes various parrot species, peccaries (wild pigs), squirrels and other arboreal mammals, and wild deer. Jaguar are also present, but these spectacular nocturnal big cats are very unlikely to be seen by the casual

Opposite: *Travellers wait to cross the border between Ecuador and Peru.*
Right: *Brightly coloured blue and yellow macaws are among the most conspicuous of hundreds of bird species to be seen along the river banks of the Amazon region and in the surrounding tropical forests and wetlands.*

visitor. The **Tumbes Reserve Zone**, which joins the Cerros de Amotape National Park on its northeast flank, comprises 751km² (290 sq miles) of wetter tropical forest, with wildlife that includes crocodiles, otters and several species of monkey.

For access to the Biosphere Reserve, contact the **Peruvian Foundation for the Conservation of Nature** (FPCN), Tarapaca 4–16, Tumbes, tel/fax: 52 34 12, e-mail: ptumbes@ mail.cosapidata.com.pe or any of the tour agencies in Tumbes and Puerto Pizarro.

AGUAS VERDES AND THE FRONTIER

The Pan-American Highway crosses the border between Peru and Ecuador at Aguas Verdes, a ramshackle settlement that exists only to service (and naturally also to profit from) cross-border traffic. The **Río Zarumilla** marks the border (which was disputed in a small and pointless war between Peru and Ecuador in 1940–41, during which Tumbes passed from Ecuadorean to Peruvian control) and is crossed by an international bridge.

Huaquillas, on the Ecuadorean side, has a handful of restaurants and some very basic guesthouses, but most travellers see little point in hanging about and travel straight onward to **Machala**, 70 km (42 miles) north of the border; to Ecuador's largest city, **Guayaquil**, 180km (105 miles) further north; or to **Cuenca**, the southern gateway to the Ecuadorean cordillera, about 175km (110 miles) east of Machala.

WILBOR TIRADO PEREZ

Artist Wilbor Tirado Perez, from Chiclayo, makes striking colourful masks of priests, warriors, demons, musicians and *arahuasceros*, inspired by ancient cultures and by the festival masks made by Peruvian villagers and city-dwellers for special occasions. He works in the National Institute of Culture in Chiclayo and some of his work is displayed in the foyer of the National Museum of Sicán (*see* page 105) near Ferreñafe.

Northern Peru at a Glance

The Gulf of Guayaquil has a hot, humid tropical climate all year round. Trujillo, Chiclayo and Lambayeque have a similar climate to the Lima region, with cool, overcast weather from May to October and warmer sunnier weather from November to April. The Cordillera Blanca has an Andean climate, with cold, dry weather from May to October and a rainy season from November to April.

Trujillo is approximately one hour's flying time from Lima, with several flights daily. There are also daily flights to Tumbes, taking just under two hours. The Pan American Highway connects Trujillo, Chiclayo, Tumbes and all points along the coast with Lima. There are several buses daily, taking around 8 hrs between Lima and Trujillo. Main bus companies include: Cruz del Sur, Jr. Amazonas 437, Trujillo, tel: 26 18 01 (Trujillo-Lima services); Emtrafesa, Av. Tupac Amaru 185, Trujillo, tel: 22 39 81 (Trujillo-Chiclayo services); El Dorado, Av. Nicolás de Pierola 1062, tel: 29 17 78 (Trujillo and Chiclayo to Máncora, Piura, Tumbes).

Local and regional express buses connect major cities and rural towns throughout the region. There are plenty of metered taxis in major towns, along with ubiquitous three-wheeled 'motos'. Cars with drivers and guides can also be chartered from tour agencies in Trujillo and Chiclayo.

Trujillo
LUXURY
Hotel El Golf, Av. de los Cocoteros 500, tel: 28 25 15, granhotelgolf@terra.com.pe The only five-star in northern Peru, with a posh restaurant and modern facilities.
Hotel Libertador Trujillo, Independencia 485, Plaza de Armas, tel: 23 27 41. Very comfortable hotel with much charm, in a colonial building on the historic main square.

MID-RANGE
Los Conquistadores Hotel, Diego de Almagro 586, tel: 20 33 50, www.losconquistadores.com Comfortable, central and affordable.

BUDGET
Hostal Solari, Diego de Almagro 715, tel: 24 39 09, hsolari@hostalsolari.com.pe Reasonably priced and well-appointed rooms.

Chiclayo
LUXURY
Grand Hotel Chiclayo, Av. Villareal 115, tel: 23 49 11, www.granhotelchiclayo.com. pe Smart modern hotel in city centre with modern facilities

including Internet access and an open-air swimming pool.

MID-RANGE
Inca Hotel Chiclayo, Luis Gonzalez 622, tel: 23 59 31, incahotel@cpi.udep.edu.pe Good value for money.

BUDGET
Costa del Sol Ramada, Av. Balta 399, tel: 22 72 72, www.costadelsolperu.com Adequate facilities and central location in Chiclayo.

Huanchaco
BUDGET
Hotel las Palmeras, Av. Larco 1150, tel: 46 11 99, www.las palmerasdehuanchaco.com On the beach, with swimming pool, restaurant and private parking.

Mancora
MID-RANGE
Las Arenas de Mancora, Las Pocitas, Mancora, tel: 85 82 40 or (Lima reservations) 441 1542, www.lasarenasde mancora.com With just 30 bungalow rooms and 300m of beachfront, there is plenty of space for everyone at this resort, which also offers kayak trips, scuba diving and other water sports, and jeep trips to the national parks and reserves of the northern region.
Villa Sirena, Playa Vichayito, Mancora, tel: 909 74 74, e-mail: reserves@ villasirenaperu.com This new resort at Vichayito beach, 1km

south of Mancora, has one of the area's best restaurants, serving imaginative dishes such as tuna carpaccio and black clam ceviche. It has a great beach and a fine choice of water sports.

WHERE TO EAT

Trujillo
LUXURY
Restaurante del Hotel el Golf, Av. Los Cocoteros 500, tel: 28 25 15.
The most elegant restaurant in the region, within the north's only five-star hotel. Excellent food and attentive service, rather formal atmosphere.

MID-RANGE
Stradivarius, Jr. Colon 327, tel: 80 84 86.
Cosy, atmospheric and clubby restaurant and café-bar serving snacks and light meals.
Huanchaco, La Mamacha, Tupac Amaru 128, tel: 46 18 01. Restaurant and pub with live Latin American music and samba, conga and tango dancing and lessons.

BUDGET
Pizzanino, Av. Juan Pablo II, 183, tel: 26 31 05.
Good, affordable pizzas, pasta and salads.
Demarco, Francisco Pizarro 725, tel: 23 42 51.
Delightful old-fashioned Italian café-restaurant, good breakfasts and lunches, excellent coffee.

Chiclayo
LUXURY
Fiesta Restaurante Gourmet, Av. Salaverry 1820, tel: 20 19 70. The best restaurant in town, with a menu offering more than 80 choices including local dishes and excellent seafood.
El Huaralino, Calle Libertad 155, tel: 27 03 30. An excellent choice for lunch, with a wide range of Chiclayan and Peruvian dishes, in the smart suburb of Santa Victoria

MID-RANGE
Las Tinaja Nortenas, Av. Las Americas 135, tel: 22 66 90. Small, lively daytime (10:00–17:00) restaurant serving typical local dishes, ten minutes' walk from the Plaza de Armas.

BUDGET
La Parra, Calle Maria Izaga 752. Two restaurants under one roof – consisting of a good 'chifa' (Chinese Peruvian) restaurant and a second kitchen preparing Chiclayo regional dishes.
Chifa Chifa, Bolognesi 769, tel: 074 20 40 21.

Peruvian-Chinese restaurant that is better than average.

Huanchaco
MID-RANGE
Huanchaco Beach, Malecon Larco 602, tel: 46 14 84. Huanchaco is known for its fish restaurants. This is one of the best, with a fine view of the bay.

TOURS AND EXCURSIONS

Alfredo Rios Mercedes, Trujillo, tel: 40 98 82, e-mail: riosmercedes@hotmail.com Personal guided tours of Chan Chan in either English, French or Spanish.
Cabalgatas Nortenas, Chiclayo, tel: 074 99 18 714. Thoroughbred horseback riding along the northern beaches or the historic trails of the Río de La Leche valley.

USEFUL CONTACTS

Tourism Information Office, Jr. Pizarro 412, Plaza de Armas, tel: 29 45 61.
LAN Peru, Jr. Francisco Pizarro 340, Trujillo, tel: 22 14 69.
LAN Peru, Manuel Maria Izaga 770, Chiclayo, tel: 074 27 48 75.

CAJAMARCA	J	F	M	A	M	J	J	A	S	O	N	D
AVERAGE TEMP. °F	71	70	70	70	71	70	70	71	71	71	72	71
AVERAGE TEMP. °C	22	21	21	21	22	21	21	22	22	22	22	22
RAINFALL in	3.6	4.2	4.6	3.4	1.7	0.5	0.2	0.3	2.3	2.3	1.9	3.2
RAINFALL mm	91	107	117	86	43	13	5	8	58	58	48	81
DAYS OF RAINFALL	13	17	17	14	9	4	2	2	9	9	8	11

7
Amazonia and the Selva

There is no greater contrast on earth than that between the soaring, snow-capped and treeless peaks and glaciers of the high Peruvian cordilleras and the utterly flat, jungle-covered selva or rainforest of Amazonia – the richest and most biodiverse tropical forest on the planet. This huge region is some 3220km (2000 miles) from the Atlantic Ocean, yet most of it is less than 120m (400ft) above sea level – more than 5000m (16,000ft) lower than the crests of the Peruvian cordilleras. Virtually all the region's communities are located along its rivers.

The jungle provinces – **Loreto**, bordering Ecuador, Colombia and Brazil; **Amazonas** and **San Martín**, between the eastern watershed of the Andes and the selva; **Ucayali**, bordering Brazil, and **Madre de Dios**, bordering both Brazil and Bolivia – share a hot and humid climate. Covering a vast area of jungle, river bank and flood-forest, they are the most thinly populated part of Peru. There are few towns and even fewer roads: until the advent of air travel, the Amazon and its tributaries were the region's main highways, and river ferries are still one of the most important means of getting around.

Three huge river systems – the **Río Ucayali**, **Río Marañón** and **Río Napo** – converge to form the **Río Amazonas** (Amazon River) close to Iquitos. The only city in the entire region, **Iquitos** is the gateway for river journeys, visits to native communities, jungle lodges and forest reserves that shelter a huge range of unique

DON'T MISS

*** **Kuélap:** lost pre-Inca city in the clouds.
*** **Jungle lodges:** stay at least a few nights in the rainforest.
** **Iquitos:** jungle city with a colourful floating market.
** **River journeys:** take a riverboat cruise down the Amazon.

Opposite: *Amerindian women in a traditional jungle house typical of Amazonia.*

wildlife, including giant otters and armadillos, pink freshwater dolphins, manatees, anacondas and river turtles, giant catfish, electric eels, harpy eagles and brilliantly coloured macaws.

CHACHAPOYAS AND AROUND

Chachapoyas, the regional capital of Amazonas province, is in the high valley of the Utcubamba River, 2335m (7500ft) above sea level in the heart of the Andean cloud-forest region. This was the heartland of the ancient Chachapoyas culture, which flourished here around the 8th–16th centuries AD, before being absorbed by the Inca.

Chachapoyas itself has little in the way of sight-seeing, but the surrounding region has plenty to reward the visitor. In addition to the great mountain citadel at **Kuélap** (*see* below) there are pre-Inca tombs at the **Laguna de Los Condores**, a 15-hour mule trek from Chachapoyas, and more tombs are carved into the cliffs of **Karajia** (near Shipata village, around 48km/30 miles west of Chachapoyas) overlooking the Juscubamba valley, a five-hour mule trek from the town.

Below: *Few visitors reach the remote fortress of Kuélap, high above the Utcubamba Valley.*

Kuélap ★★★

Kuélap, 72km (44 miles) from Chachapoyas, is amazingly seldom visited. Built in the 9th century AD and rediscovered in 1843, this was the main **citadel** of the Chachapoyas culture and covers around 6ha (14 acres) of hillside overlooking the deep Utcubamba valley, at an altitude of 3000m (9840 ft). Ringed with massive stone **defensive walls**, Kuélap has some 420 **circular stone buildings**, many with conical thatched roofs, and its walls are decorated with geometric friezes. The **ramparts** are up to 25m (82ft) in height and are pierced by three narrow **gates** that permit only one person at a time to enter.

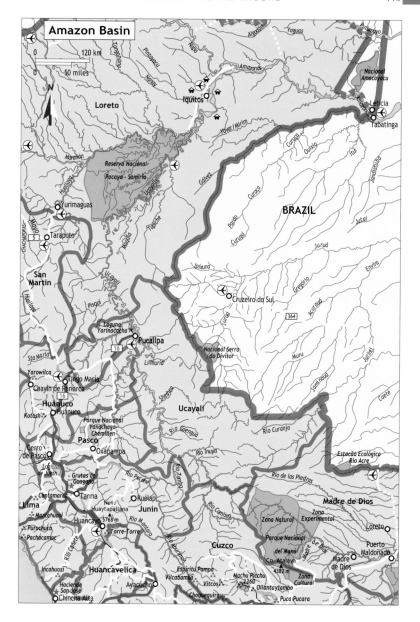

Above: *The best way to explore the forests of the Amazon region is by boat.*
Opposite: *Scarlet macaws are among the most colourful parrot species in the Amazon forests.*

RUBBER

The rubber tree – native to Amazonia and originally found nowhere else – brought great wealth to the Iquitos rubber merchants when industrialization brought a boom in demand in the second half of the 19th century. Native people were enslaved at gunpoint to work as rubber tappers and many died of hunger, disease and abuse. The Amazon traders lost their monopoly on rubber when a British botanist smuggled seeds of the rubber tree to London and British planters began growing rubber in Malaya, while German scientists invented synthetic rubber.

Iquitos **

Iquitos owes its existence to the Amazon and the 19th-century rubber boom, when its merchants made fortunes from the 'white gold' of Amazonia and built extravagant mansions and public buildings, some of which survive today. It also has the unlikely distinction of being the largest city to be inaccessible by road from the outside world – a 200km (125-mile) stretch of highway connects it with Nauta, further up the Río Marañón, but to go anywhere else you must travel by plane or riverboat. The town forms a geometric grid of streets behind the **Malecon** (where some of the grandest 19th-century buildings survive), with the bank of the **River Amazon** to the east and the **Plaza de Armas**, the centre of the original settlement, a couple of blocks inland. Iquitos was founded by Jesuit missionaries in 1750, but remained (literally) a backwater settlement of fewer than 2000 people until the rubber boom reached the Peruvian Amazon in the 1870s, when its population soared to almost 30,000.

The end of the golden age of the rubber traders relegated it again to backwater status, until the discovery of **oil reserves** in the region brought a new wave of prosperity in the second half of the 20th century. For the visitor, Amazon river journeys, jungle lodges and nature reserves hold more allure than Iquitos itself, but this surprisingly cosmopolitan jungle capital does have undeniable character and an array of attractions of its own. The best known, and definitely the most interesting, is the **floating market** quarter of **Belem**, on the south side of town, where more than 7000 people live and work in huts, sheds and shops of wood, thatch and corrugated iron, floating on makeshift pontoons. The market is a glorious conglomeration of shacks and stalls selling everything from household goods and staple supplies to such exotica as piranha teeth, turtle shells, weird charms and herbal remedies, and much more. The **Iron House**, the most famous relic of Iquitos's glory days, was designed by Gustav Eiffel (of Eiffel Tower fame) and imported from France by river boat, to be assembled piece by piece like a giant construction toy. Located at the southeast corner of the Plaza de Armas, it is now a café-restaurant.

Around Iquitos, several lakes and river lagoons can be visited by motorboat; **Laguna Moronacocha**, the nearest to town, is also accessible by *colectivo* or taxi. **Santo Tomás**, **Santa Clara** and **Corientillo**, 15–16km (10 miles) from Iquitos, are lakeside villages on lagoons formed by the **Río Nanay**. All three have small riverside bars and restaurants, and there are places to swim at Santa Clara and Corientillo.

Further afield, the best way to experience the Amazon forest is to stay at one of the jungle lodges (*see* Where to Stay, page 120) that are dotted along river banks 40km (25 miles) to 160km (100 miles) from Iquitos and connected to the city by high-speed river launches. From these bases, visitors can make guided treks into the forest. A unique attraction, 160km (100 miles) from Iquitos on the Río Napo, is the **ACTS Field Station** with its vertiginous web of jungle-canopy walkways 35m (105ft) above ground level. Cruises on the Amazon are also offered on purpose-built vessels including the *Río Amazonas* (with air-conditioned luxury suites) which sails on weekly itineraries from Iquitos, cruising down to Leticia on the Brazilian border and back.

Pacaya Samiria National Reserve ***

Nauta, around 105km (66 miles) south of Iquitos (three hours by car, by the only road through the jungle) and close to the confluence of the Río Marañón and Río Ucayali, is mainly of interest as a gateway to the Pacaya Samiria National Reserve, which is named after the two rivers which flow through it.

This 2,000,000ha (5,000,000-acre) expanse of jungle rivers, lagoons and swamps forms a huge triangle of territory between the Marañón and the Ucayali and provides a refuge for river

---

PARK GUIDELINES

• Visit only authorized areas.
• Do not interfere with scientific research activities.
• Do not establish contact with native communities.
• Do not collect flora and fauna.
• Respect Park Authority regulations and advice from park rangers.

AYAHUASCA

Ayahuasca is a powerful natural hallucinogenic drink, prepared from an Amazonian vine by an *ayahuascero* who guides the drinker through the drug experience, which can include vivid visions and which lasts for around four hours. *Ayahuasca* is not an illegal drug, but experimenters should be aware that like many natural hallucinogens it can have unwelcome side effects including nausea.

PEOPLE OF THE MANÚ

The protected forests of the Manú National Park and its fringes are home to several of Peru's indigenous jungle-dwelling peoples, each with their own traditions, language and way of life. They include communities of Mashiguenga, Amahuaca, Yaminahua, Piro, Amarakaeri, Huashipari and Nahua people. A few villages welcome visitors; most, however are inaccessible, or off limits to tourists.

Below: *Thick virgin forest canopy covers the valleys and foothills of the Manú National Park.*

dolphins, manatee, anaconda, giant charapa turtles, jaguar and dozens of bird species. Known as the 'mirror jungle' because of the dazzling reflections of sky and forest in its still waters, this is the largest flood forest in Amazonia and can be explored by boat with a guide from Nauta or from Bretana (on a tributary of the Ucayali, about one day by river boat from Iquitos) or Lagunas (on the Río Huallaga). Allow up to seven days for a visit to Pacaya Samiria, as the outskirts are less rich in wildlife and it takes at least one day to travel into the heart of the park.

PUCALLPA *

Pucallpa, capital of Ucayali province, has the air of a frontier town, with dirt streets and shabby modern concrete buildings. This river port on the Río Ucayali is, literally, the end of the road: river ferries leave regularly for Iquitos, taking three to five days to complete the journey. **Lake Yarinacocha**, 8km (5 miles) northeast of Pucallpa, is a branch of the Ucayali that is cut off from the river in the dry season. On its banks are several Shipibo Indian villages, and the lake shelters a variety of wildlife. The small lakeside village of **Puerto Callao** has a number of basic guest-houses and eating places, and boats can be hired to explore the lake.

Manú National Park ***

The Manú National Park is the largest protected natural area in Peru and one of the largest in the world, covering 1,716,295 ha (4,300,000 acres) of foothills and rainforest and straddling the regional boundaries of Cuzco and Madre de Dios provinces. The reserve stretches from the eastern watershed of the Andes, 4000m (13,124ft) above sea level, to the flatlands of the Manú river basin, only 250m (820ft) above sea level, and embraces a huge variety of environments and ecosystems. The heartland of the park is off limits to non-scientists, while a reserved area is open to visitors, and villages and farming are permitted on the outer fringes. Declared a UNESCO Biosphere Reserve in 1977, Manú became a World Natural Heritage Site in 1987. More than 800 species of birds – including the harpy eagle, the jabiru, jungle goose and cock-of-the-rocks – are found in the Manú region, along with more than 200 mammal species including monkeys, deer, giant river otter,

ocelot, jaguar, spectacled bear and more than 100 kinds of bat. The incredible diversity of plant species ranges from giant orchids and tropical hardwood trees reaching up to 45m (150ft) tall and 3m (9ft) thick to ferns and saprophytes. Many of the region's reptile and insect species have yet to be classified.

Above: *Boats like these canoes bringing villagers to market at Puerto Maldonado are the only way of travelling around the region.*

Specialist companies (*see* At a Glance, page 121) offer guided tours with equipment included, jungle trekking, river rafting and visits to some of the native communities. Allow at least five days as travel is slow and the park is huge.

PUERTO MALDONADO

Like Iquitos, Puerto Maldonado – last stop on the Río Madre de Dios before the Bolivian border – grew up as a rubber boom town in the late 19th century. It is now a river port and agricultural centre, and the jumping-off point for some interesting river journeys along the **Río Madre de Dios** and the **Río Heath** (which marks the border between Peru and Bolivia). The **Tambopata National Reserve** and the adjoining **Bahuaja Sonene National Park**, two hours south of Puerto Maldonado, offer jungle lodges, river journeys, trekking, camping, and bird and wildlife watching within a combined area of more than 1,214,100ha (3 million acres) of subtropical rainforest. The jungle lakes, **Lago Sandoval** and **Lago Valencia**, both around two hours from Puerto Maldonado, are also well worth visiting, with rich wildlife, jungle trails and lodges to stay in.

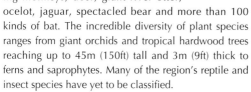

COLONEL FAWCETT

Percy Harrison Fawcett (1867–1925?) is one of the legends of South American exploration. In 1906 the Brazilian, Peruvian and Bolivian governments jointly asked the Royal Geographical Society in London to provide a surveyor to define their jungle frontiers. Fawcett, an officer in the Royal Artillery, got the job and spent years mapping the unexplored terrain of the border regions. After World War I, he returned to Amazonia, making several expeditions into jungles of the Matto Grosso, where in 1925 he vanished – never to be heard from again, despite occasional rumours that he was living as chief of a native tribe.

Amazonia and the Selva at a Glance

Chachapoyas/Kuélap: Rain is rare Jun–Oct. Temperatures are mild to cold, year round.

Iquitos: Nov–Mar is the least humid season but heat and humidity are high all year round and heavy rain is possible at any time.

Manú and Puerto Maldonado: May–Oct is the best time to visit. Days can be very hot (up to 32ºC/90ºF), though the nights are cooler; frequent rain is possible at any time of year. Occasional chill katabatic winds from the Andes, known as *friajes*, occasionally push temperatures below 10ºC (50ºF).

There are very few roads in the Amazon region and little or no public surface transport. For the visitor to this area, the most realistic option is to **fly** as travel by road is difficult and very time consuming.

Chachapoyas/Kuélap: Flights from Lima via Tarapoto (90 minutes).

Iquitos: Daily flights from Lima (1 hour) and Pucallpa (50 minutes). The river journey from Pucallpa takes six days.

Manú National Park: Light aircraft can be chartered to fly from Cuzco to Boca Manú, where the Río Manú joins the Madre de Dios. The boat trip into the Manú National Park takes 4–8 hours.

Puerto Maldonado: There are flights at least daily to Lima via Cuzco. Its is possible to travel by truck from Cuzco in the drier season but the journey takes at least three days.

In the Chachapoyas region, four-wheel-drive vehicles and drivers can be chartered privately. There is very little public transport. Mules and muleteers can also be hired for treks to Laguna de los Condores and Karaija. Distances in the Amazon basin are vast and the most convenient way to travel within the region is undoubtedly by light aircraft. From Iquitos, fast river launches take guests to the jungle lodges, within a 100km (60-mile) radius of the city. For those with more time to spend, travel by river boat between Iquitos and Pucallpa or further down the Amazon, or from Puerto Maldonado both up and down the Río Madre de Dios, can be a rewarding way of seeing riverside communities and experiencing river life.

Chachapoyas
MID-RANGE
Hotel Gran Vilaya,
Ayacucho 755, Chachapoyas, tel: (041) 77 76 64.
Modern and functional hotel, with its own café.

Hotel Casa Viega, Jr. Chincha Alta, Chachapoyas, tel: (041) 77 73 53, www.casaviejaperu.com Cosy, comfortable and stylish family-run hotel with a good restaurant, in a charming 19th-century traditional mansion house.

Iquitos
LUXURY
Eldorado Plaza,
Napo 258, Iquitos, tel: (065) 22 25 55, www. eldoradoplazahotel.com With five stars, this is the best (and most expensive) hotel in town, with luxuries including a pool, gym, and sauna.

Explorama Lodges,
Av. La Marina 340, Iquitos, tel: (065) 25 25 30, www.explorama.com This is a group of six lodges located around 40–160km (25–100 miles) from Iquitos, with high-speed river launch shuttles; the group includes the ACTS Field Station lodge and the Explornapo lodge near the jungle canopy walkway. Accommodation and facilities include such luxuries as air conditioning, en-suite bathrooms, and a swimming pool.

MID-RANGE
Hotel Victoria Regia,
Ricardo Palma 252, tel: (065) 23 19 83, www.victoriaregia hotel.com Comfortable and well-run, with a pool and its own restaurant.

Amazonia and the Selva at a Glance

BUDGET
Hotel Marañón,
tel: (084) 24 26 73, e-mail:
hotel.maranon@terra.com.pe
The newest hotel in Iquitos
with excellent facilities and
rooms at affordable rates.

Puerto Maldonado
LUXURY
Libertador Tambopata Lodge,
Tambopata National Reserve,
tel: (084) 24 56 95,
www.tambopatalodge.com
This is the most luxurious
lodge in the reserve, with a
good choice of wildlife
viewing trips.

MID-RANGE
Estancia Bello Horizonte,
Av. do de Mayo 287, Puerto
Maldonado, tel: (082) 57 27
48, www.estanciabello
horizonte.com
Comfortable lodge with
thatched bungalows and
pool; offers jungle treks and
river journeys.
Sandoval Lake Lodge,
Tambopata Natural Reserve,
www.inkanatura.com
The only lodge overlooking
this protected oxbow lake
within the Tambopata
Natural Reserve.

BUDGET
Residencial Amarumayo,
Libertad 433, Puerto Maldonada, tel: (082) 57 38 60.
Comfortable, with pool, its
own arts and crafts gallery,
restaurant and resident traditional dance troupe.

WHERE TO EAT

Iquitos has a surprisingly
good choice of restaurants of
all sorts, including several
serving fresh river fish.
Iquitos and Puerto
Maldonado also have plenty
of small cafés and juice bars
serving freshly squeezed fruit
juices, as well as pizzerias,
snack bars and even a few
Chinese restaurants. Away
from the main towns, the
only options are the jungle
lodge restaurants, which
serve a choice of inter-
national dishes, Peruvian
favourites and fresh river fish.

TOURS AND EXCURSIONS

Inkaterra, Andalucia 174,
Lima, tel: (01) 610 0404,
www.inkaterra.com
Treks, expeditions and jungle
lodges throughout Amazonia,
including the ACTS jungle
canopy walkway near Iquitos.

Aracari Tours, Av. Pardo 610,
Miraflores, Lima, tel: (01) 242
6673, www.aracari.com
This tour operator offers
4–8-day itineraries around
Chachapoyas, including treks
to Laguna de Los Condores
and Leymebamba.

Peruvian Safaris,
Av. Leon Velarde 153,
Puerto Maldonado,
www.peruviansafaris.com
Journeys into the Tambopata
National Reserve, jungle
lodge accommodation,
river journeys.

Rainforest Expeditions,
Av. Aeropuerto Km 6,
La Joya, Puerto Maldonado,
tel: (082) 52 55 75,
www.perunature.com
Treks, lodges and river
journeys.

USEFUL CONTACTS

Chachapoyas Tourist Office,
Junín 801.
Iquitos Tourist Office, Napo
232, tel: (065) 23 56 21.
**Puerto Maldonado Tourist
Office**, Fitcarraldo 252, tel:
(082) 57 14 13.
National Park Office (Inrena),
Cuzco 135, Puerto Maldo-
nado, tel: (082) 57 16 04.
AeroCondor, Jr Loreto 222,
Plaza de Armas,
tel: 57 17 33, www.
aerocondor.pe Flights to
Puerto Maldonado from
Arequipa and Iquitos from
Cuzco with connections
to/from Lima.

AMAZON BASIN	J	F	M	A	M	J	J	A	S	O	N	D
AVERAGE TEMP. °F	85	86	85	86	83	80	81	87	91	88	88	86
AVERAGE TEMP. °C	29	30	29	30	28	27	27	31	33	31	31	30
RAINFALL in	7.6	6.1	4.6	2.4	3.1	0.9	1.1	0.6	2.3	3	8.1	5.2
RAINFALL mm	193	155	117	61	79	23	28	15	58	76	206	132
DAYS OF RAINFALL	15	13	12	5	6	4	2	4	4	8	11	15

Travel Tips

Tourist Information

Tourist information is provided by the **Peruvian Tourist Board** (www.peru.info) in Lima, and by embassies and consulates outside of Peru. These are: **Australia:** 3rd Floor, 30 Clarence Street, Sydney, NSW 2000, tel: 02 9262 6464;
Canada: 130 Albert Street, Suite 1901, Ottawa, Ontario, Canada, K1P 5G4, tel: 613 238 1777;
United Kingdom: 52 Sloane Street, London SW1X 9SP, tel: 020 7235 1917;
United States of America: 3001 Garrison Street NW, Washington DC 20008, tel: 202 363 4808;
Other countries: information and tourism literature may be obtained from the Peruvian embassy or consulate.
Within Peru: Commission for the Promotion of Peru, Calle Uno Oeste #050, piso 13, Urb. Córpac, San Isidro, Lima, tel: 224 3131, www.promperu.gob.pe

Entry Requirements

Visas are not required by nationals of the USA, UK, Canada, Australia, New Zealand, Germany and most other British Commonwealth and European Union nations for a stay of up to 90 days. Your passport should have six months' validity on arrival. Make sure you keep hold of your Embarkation/Disembarkation card during your stay, and this is needed on departure.

Customs

You may import three litres of alcohol, 400 cigarettes, or 50 cigars, or 250 grams of tobacco, and gifts to a value of up to US \$300. It is forbidden to take historical artefacts out of the country, or anything made of endangered animal skin or shell.

Health Requirements

A yellow fever vaccination, administered 10 days before travelling, is required for those coming from a yellow fever infected area, or for those intending to visit the jungle areas. Immunization against tetanus, diphtheria and hepatitis A are recommended, as is a malaria preventative.

Getting There

By Air: The main flight connections from Europe are with Iberia Airlines via Madrid and KLM via Amsterdam-Schiphol. There are also direct flights to Peru from North America, with the main airlines being American Airlines and Air Canada. The international airport in Peru is Jorge Chávez Airport in Lima.
By Land: Cruz del Sur bus company offers bus services between Peru and Ecuador, to the north and Chile, to the south.
By Sea: There are regular cruise trips from the United States to Callao in Peru.
By River: It is possible to travel to Iquitos, in the centre of Peru's jungle provinces, by river ferry on the Amazon from Brazil. River ferries also connect the southern river port of Puerto Maldonado, on the Río Madre de Dios, with Bolivia.

What to Pack

In the dry season (May to September) the days are sunny, but the nights are usually cold, so warm fleece gear is recommended. If you are planning on heading into the mountains, waterproof clothing should be taken. Good walking boots are essential for the Inca Trail and the highlands. Other items of use include a Swiss Army knife (packed into checked baggage while travelling), a good mosquito repellent (essential for the Amazon regions), binoculars, and a small torch and batteries. Tablets for sterilizing tap water are also highly recommended.

Money Matters

Currency: The Peruvian Nuevo Sol (Sl) is divided into 100 céntimos. Coins come in denominations of 5, 10, 20 and 50 céntimos. Notes are in denominations of 10, 20, 50, 100 and 200 Nuevos Soles. US dollars are often accepted in major tourist establishments and larger restaurants.
Exchange: It is possible to pay with US dollars as well as soles in many places, but small bills are preferred – keep a supply of $1 and $5 bills handy. Sterling notes are difficult to exchange except in large city banks. Dollar and euro notes can be changed in most places (in the Miraflores district of Lima street money-changers can be identified by their maroon-coloured jerkins) and money-changers stay open until late. In major cities and towns, automatic teller machines (ATMs) can be used to withdraw cash using credit or debit cards compat-

ible with the Maestro and Cirrus systems. Travellers cheques are difficult to change outside major cities, even in tourist hotels.
Tipping: Restaurants usually add a service charge (*servicio*) of between 5 and 10 percent to the bill, but an additional tip can be paid if the service warrants it. Tour guides should also be tipped, but taxi drivers should not.

Road Signs

Road signs are in Spanish, distances are in kilometres, and speed limits are in kilometres per hour.

Accommodation

Accommodation in Peru ranges from five-star luxury hotels in Lima and at the more popular tourist hot-spots such as Cuzco to very simple hotels and guesthouses. Most major towns have comfortable three-star hotels as well, and rates are very affordable by European and North American standards at all levels of accommodation. In the cheapest hotels, do not expect frills such as air conditioning, en-suite bathrooms or even hot water. In the Amazon regions, jungle lodges offer comfortable, simple accommodation but prices are relatively high as all supplies of fuel, food and drink must be shipped in by river boat. On the islands of Lake Titicaca, it is possible to stay in local family homes at a very low price, but comforts are minimal and a sleeping bag is essential.

PUBLIC HOLIDAYS AND FESTIVALS

1 January • New Year's Day
February • Carnaval
February • Virgen de la Candelaria (Puno)
Week before Easter • Semana Santa
1 May • Fiesta de la Cruz and Labour Day
24 June • Inti Raymi (Cuzco)
29 June • San Pedro y San Pablo
28–29 July • Día de la Independencia del Peru
30 August • Santa Rosa de Lima
8 October • Battle of Angamos
20 October • Procession of the Lord of Miracles
1 November • Todos los Santos (All Saints Day)
8 December • Día de la Inmaculada Concepción
25 December • Christmas Day

Eating Out

Peru has plenty of restaurants around the country, and even if some of them seem overly simple affairs, the food is generally very good. In the coastal regions fish is the natural speciality, including *ceviche* (marinated raw fish) and *camarones* (prawn stew). Inland food is more hearty, making much use of potatoes and corn, such as *tamales* (meat-filled corn dumplings). Beef and goat (kid) are also abundant. International food options include pizza and pasta restaurants, burger bars, and a surprising number of Peruvian-Chinese restaurants

Candelaria, the Festival of the Virgin of the Candle, is one of the most important annual religious events in Peru. In Puno, more than 30,000 dancers and 8000 musicians gather for the event, which begins on 2 February with a huge procession of dancers in jewelled costumes and beribboned hats, guised as condors and llama keepers. The event reaches a crescendo on 8 February with dancers in heavily embroidered cloaks and grotesque demonic masks parading through the streets.

that make their appearance in even quite out-of-the-way towns – though their menu would not be instantly recognizable to a visitor from Hong Kong or Beijing.

Transport

Air: Peru has more than 50 regional airports – many of them no more than airstrips in the jungle or the desert – and

flying is the only realistic way of covering the long distances between major sights on a relatively short holiday, as a journey that takes no more than an hour by air can take 20 hours or more by road. There are frequent domestic air services between Lima and all other major cities as well as some of the remote small towns in the Amazon region. Several Peruvian domestic airlines have ceased operating in recent years. Survivors include Chilean-owned LAN and the independent airline AeroCondor, which has expanded to become the country's biggest domestic airlines. Safety standards appear to have improved somewhat in recent years, with fewer accidents reported, and it should be noted that surface transport in Peru also has a poor safety record.

Trains: Train travel is not widespread in Peru, but there are two popular tourist train routes – one from Puno to Cuzco, and another from Cuzco to Machu Picchu, via Ollantaytambo.

Buses: Buses are the best way of getting to many parts of Peru, and comfortable, frequent and efficient long-haul buses cover all regions of the country except the remote Amazon. Roads are generally good, and long-distance express buses have reclining seats and air conditioning.

Car hire: An international driver's licence is required and should be carried at all times, as well as the rental contract. Speed limits are indicated on signposts on highways. Traffic officers wear a uniform and ID. Under no circumstance pull over if a stranger signals you to stop, nor allow anyone to get into your car under the pretext of being traffic police. Official traffic police are not allowed to get into your car.

Taxis: Only use private taxi firms booked by phone, or municipal yellow taxis in Lima. Negotiate the price prior to the journey because Peruvian taxis have no meters.

Business Hours

Banks are normally open from 09:00–18:00 Mon–Fri, and from 09:00–12:00 Sat. Most government and commercial offices are open from 09:30–17:00. Shops and craft markets are usually open daily between 09:00 and 20:00.

Time Difference

GMT –5 hours.

Communications

Post offices: Post office opening hours are usually 09:00–18:00 and they can be

CONVERSION CHART		
FROM	**TO**	**MULTIPLY BY**
Millimetres	Inches	0.0394
Metres	Yards	1.0936
Metres	Feet	3.281
Kilometres	Miles	0.6214
Square kilometres	Square miles	0.386
Hectares	Acres	2.471
Litres	Pints	1.760
Kilograms	Pounds	2.205
Tonnes	Tons	0.984
To convert Celsius to Fahrenheit: x 9 ÷ 5 + 32		

found in most towns, usually on or around the Plaza de Armas. There is also an efficient Poste Restante service in Peru where tourists can pick up mail addressed to them at post offices.

Telephones: It is possible to make national and international calls from pay phones. Pay phones accept coins and phone cards that are sold at kiosks and in some supermarkets. Avoid making phone calls from hotels, because the price will be astronomical. The directory enquiry number (in Spanish) is 103. Mobile phone networks operate in the main cities.

Internet: Internet facilities (cabinas pública) are now available in most Peruvian towns and cities.

Electricity

220 volts, although some four- and five-star hotels use 110 volts. Volt transformers can be bought in Peru. Two-pin, flat-blade plugs are used.

Weights and Measures

Peru uses the metric system of measurement.

Health Precautions

Make sure you have comprehensive health insurance prior to travelling to Peru. Do not drink tap water anywhere in Peru unless you have boiled or sterilized it yourself. Carry water sterilizing tablets, available from chemists in the UK, and elsewhere, if you are heading off the beaten track where bottled drinks may not

be available. Avoid eating from street food stalls, and be careful when eating raw vegetables and fruits that may have been washed in local tap water. Pack Immodium or a similar preparation to alleviate symptoms of diarrhoea, as well as electrolyte mix for rehydration. A particular health risk in Peru is altitude sickness (soroche). This can be prevented by travelling to the higher regions in stages and by resting on your first day in the highlands. Drinking coca leaf tea can alleviate mild symptoms of altitude sickness, such as faintness and headaches. The more serious symptoms of altitude sickness should be dealt with by descending to lower ground immediately.

Health Services

Most four- or five-star hotels should have contact details for doctors on call, and your travel insurance should cover you in the event of emergency repatriation. The emergency hospital in Lima is the Hospital de Emergencias José Casimiro Ulloa, Avenue Roosevelt #6355, Miraflores, Lima 18, tel: 241 2789 or 445 5096.

Personal Safety

Most of Peru is a safe travel destination, particularly within the tourist regions, but normal common sense should apply, particularly with regard to pickpockets in the larger cities. They mainly operate in crowded areas,

USEFUL SPANISH PHRASES

Hello • Hola
How are you? • ¿Cómo está usted?
Please • Por favor
Thank you • Gracias
Yes/No • Si/No
How much? • ¿Cuánto es?
Bus • Autobús
Train • Tren
Hotel • Hotel
1 • uno
2 • dos
3 • tres
4 • cuatro
5 • cinco
6 • seis
7 • siete
8 • ocho
9 • nueve
10 • diez

such as markets, and bus stations. It is also inadvisable to carry any luggage on your back for the same reasons. All valuables should be placed in a hotel safety deposit box, but carry a photocopy of your passport and any other identification papers with you at all times. If a safety deposit box is not an option, carry valuables in a secure money belt or concealed pouch. All visitors, but especially women, should avoid walking alone at night. Any political demonstrations should be avoided, and particular care should also be taken in the Huaraz region near Huayhuash.

Emergencies

Ambulance (SAMU): 117
Fire: 116
Police: 105

Tourist emergency number: 424 2053

Etiquette

Peruvians are fairly laid-back people and there are no great formalities to behaviour here, although a handshake is always expected on greeting, and common courtesy applies. Dress is informal in all but the most chic of places. Although there are no strict codes, modest dress, such as covered tops of arms and mid-length shorts or skirts are recommended when visiting churches and other religious sites. Smoking is fairly widespread.

Language

Both Spanish and Quechua are official languages in Peru, but the majority of the population speak Spanish. The Aymará language is mainly spoken in the Lake Titicaca region. In the main tourist regions English is generally understood.

Shopping

The real draw for shoppers in Peru is the wonderful array of distinctive handicrafts. Rugs and knitwear made from alpaca wool, silver jewellery, tapestries and eerie-looking Indian masks are all good buys and not too difficult to transport home. In Lima the main shopping area for handicrafts in both shops and markets is the Miraflores district. But, particularly in the most touristy areas, street vendors will be found everywhere, and their prices are likely to be cheaper than in the capital. In markets, bargaining is an acceptable means of negotiating a price. Regional specialities include traditional woven baskets and tribal jewellery in the Amazon (as well as spears, which may be more problematic at customs), coca leaf tea (mate) from the Andean regions, and ceramics in Arequipa. Note that the purchase of historical artefacts or of items made out of endangered animal skin or turtleshell is illegal.

GOOD READING

Alegria, Ciro, *The Golden Serpent*, Signet/New American Library. Recently republished novel of life in an Andean village by one of Peru's greatest 20th-century novelists.
Bingham, Hiram, *Lost City of the Incas*, Weidenfeld & Nicholson.
Cotterell, Maurice, *The Lost Tomb of Viracocha*, Headline. Unlocks the secrets of the Viracocha tombs and the Tihuanaco civilization.
Daniel, AB, *The Gold of Cuzco* and *The Light of Machu Pichu* (both Pocket Books, www.simonsays.co.uk). New trilogy of historical novels set during the decline and fall of the Inca Empire. Mario Vargas Llosa
de la Vega, Garcilaso Inca, *The Incas*, Andean World. The classic account of the rise and fall of the Inca civilization.
Deary, Terry, *The Incredible Incas*, Hippo. Inca history for kids, with the gory bits left in.
Guevara, Che, *The Motorcycle Diaries*, 4th Estate. The legendary guerrilla's account of the journey through South America that shaped his revolutionary beliefs.
Murphy, Dervla, *Eight Feet in the Andes: Travels with a Mule in Unknown Peru*, John Murray.
Shaffer, Peter, *The Royal Hunt of the Sun*, Penguin.
Simpson, Joe, *Touching the Void*, Jonathan Cape.
Vargas Llosa, Mario, *Conversation in the Cathedral*, Rayo.
Vargas Llosa, Mario, *Death in the Andes*, Faber & Faber.
Vargas Llosa, Mario, Complete works of Peru's best-known author have recently been reissued (in English) by Faber and Faber, including *The Feast of the Goat*, *Making Waves*, *Aunt Julia and the Scriptwriter*, *The Way to Paradise*, *The Time of the Hero*, and *The War of the End of the World*.
Wilder, Thornton, *The Bridge of San Luis Rey*, Perennial.